Along the Hudson and Mohawk

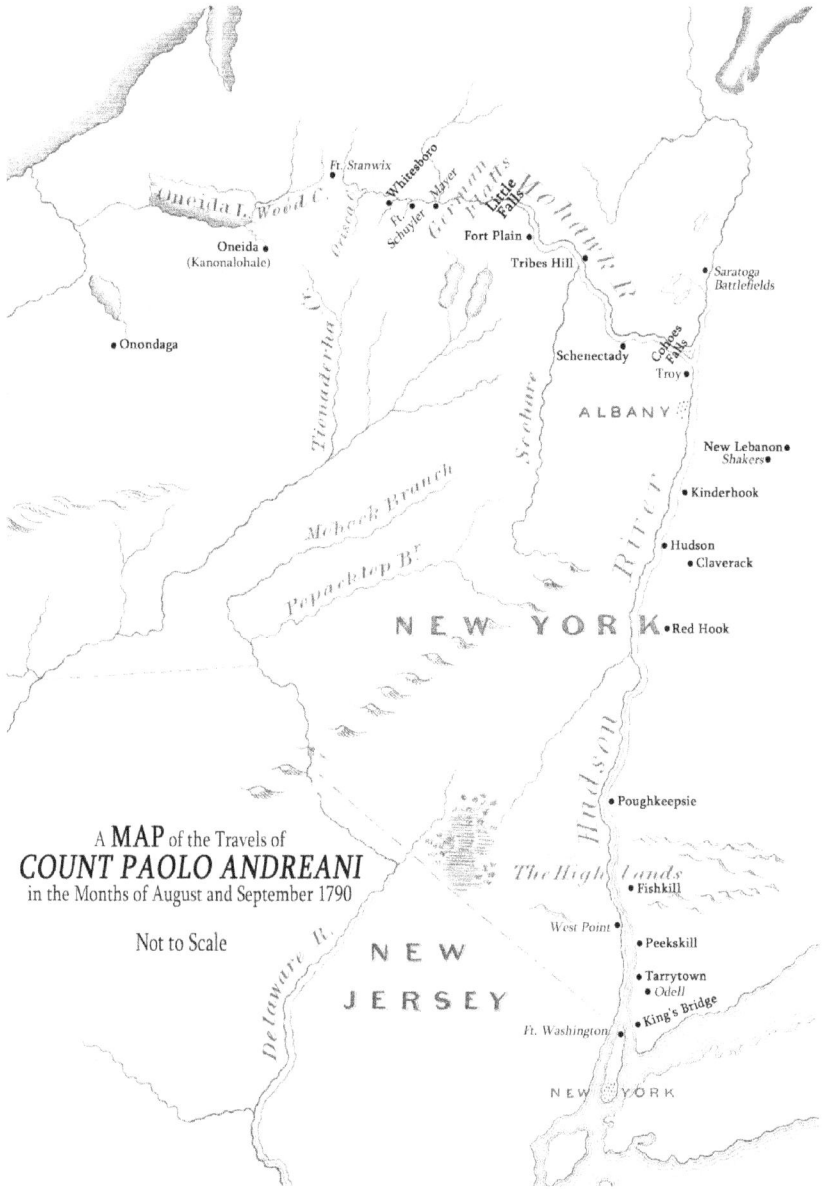

Ft. Stanwix
Whitesboro
Mayer
Ft. Schuyler
Oneida L. Wood C.
German Flatts
Little Falls
Mohawk R.
Fort Plain
Oneida
(Kanonalohale)
Tribes Hill
Saratoga Battlefields
Onondaga
Tionaderha
Schoharie
Schenectady
Cohoes Falls
Troy
ALBANY
New Lebanon
Shakers
Kinderhook
Mohawk Branch
Papacktop Br
Hudson
Claverack
NEW YORK
Red Hook
Hudson River
Poughkeepsie

A MAP of the Travels of
COUNT PAOLO ANDREANI
in the Months of August and September 1790

Not to Scale

The High Lands
Fishkill
West Point
Peekskill
Delaware R.
NEW JERSEY
Tarrytown
Odell
King's Bridge
Ft. Washington
NEW YORK

Along the Hudson and Mohawk

The 1790 Journey of Count Paolo Andreani

TRANSLATED AND EDITED BY
CESARE MARINO AND
KARIM M. TIRO

Iroquoian linguistic notes by
Roy A. Wright (Tekastiaks)

PENN

University of Pennsylvania Press

Philadelphia

10 9 8 7 6 5 4 3 2 1

Published by
University of Pennsylvania Press
Philadelphia, Pennsylvania 19104-4112

Library of Congress Cataloging-in-Publication Data

Andreani, Paolo, 1763–1823.
    [Giornale 1790. English]
    Along the Hudson and Mohawk : the 1790 journey of Count Paolo Andreani /
translated and edited by Cesare Marino and Karim M. Tiro ; Iroquoian linguistic
notes by Roy A. Wright (Tekastiaks)
        p. cm.
    Includes selected letters, 1790–1791.
    Includes bibliographical references and index.
    ISBN-13: 978-0-8122-3914-0
    ISBN-10: 0-8122-3914-8 (cloth : alk. paper)
    1. New York (State)—Description and travel—Early works to 1800. 2. Hudson
River (N.Y. and N.J.)—Description and travel—Early works to 1800. 3. Mohawk River
(N.Y.)—Description and travel—Early works to 1800. 4. Indians of North America—
New York (State)—History—18th century. 5. Andreani, Paolo, 1763–1823—Travel—
New York (State) 6. Italians—Travel—New York (State)—History—18th century.
I. Marino, Cesare R. (Cesare Rosario). II. Tiro, Karim M. III. Andreani, Paolo,
1763–1823. Correspondence. English. Selections. IV. Title.

F123.A5313 2006
917.47′1042—dc22
                                                                2005042366

Frontispiece: A map of the travels of Count Paolo Andreani in the months of
August and September 1790. Adapted by Tina Meagher, Cesare Marino,
and Karim M. Tiro from E. B. O'Callaghan, *Documentary History of the State
of New-York*, vol. 1 (Albany: Weed and Parsons, 1851).

Permit me to introduce to you . . . a young nobleman from Milan. You will find him well informed on many subjects . . . and not more recommended to your esteem by his science, than he is by his agreeable manners to your civilities.

—James Madison to Benjamin Rush, July 5, 1790

Count Andreani is just such a man as you have described him to be in your letter. Is it not disgraceful to our country to suffer its natural productions to be explored and described only by foreigners?

—Benjamin Rush to James Madison, July 17, 1790

Contents

Preface

From mid-August to mid-September 1790, Count Paolo Andreani of Milan undertook an overland journey through New York State and eastern Iroquoia. Andreani kept a journal of his observations of the human and physical landscape, as well as the daily details of his progress up the Hudson and Mohawk rivers. He likely intended to publish it in some form, for afterward he produced a partially edited, annotated, and illustrated version, copied out carefully in his own best hand. Although the journal never appeared in print, the manuscript may well have circulated among members of his family and his network of personal acquaintances in Italy. Because there is no evidence of its translation into French or English, however, it is unlikely that it circulated among his wider circle of correspondents, which included Francisco de Miranda and the Duke de la Rochefoucauld-Liancourt.

No copies of Andreani's original field notes seem to have survived. Nor, with a single exception, have the illustrations alluded to in the text. They may have been seized by the count's many unhappy creditors. Alternatively, they may have sunk in the Atlantic along with some minerals Andreani sent his brother on an ill-fated vessel; or in a New York river when Andreani's sled fell through the ice, taking with it papers, scientific instruments, and three horses. However, Andreani's fair copy of his travel journal, which runs to 119 numbered pages, survived, and some time in the twentieth century it became the possession (along with several other Andreani journals and papers) of one of Andreani's descendants, Count Antonio Sormani Verri of Milan. In the early 1950s, Count Sormani authorized Professor Antonio Pace, who was then conducting research in Italy, to have the *Giornale 1790* microfilmed. Subsequently, as a symbolic return of Count Andreani to America, Pace deposited a microfilm copy of the document in the collections of the American Philosophical Society in Philadelphia, of which

Andreani had been elected a member more than a century and a half earlier. Until today, the *Giornale* has remained virtually unknown and unused and it has never before been translated, edited, and annotated in its entirety.

We have also reproduced a number of Andreani's American letters to his friend Miranda and his brother, Gian Mario Andreani. They provide valuable information about those parts of Andreani's visit to America outside the period covered by his journal. These letters also include observations and opinions that Andreani felt inappropriate for his journal. This volume ends with Andreani's departure for Canada in 1791. We are presently collecting the fragments of his extant writings from the remainder of his travels, which took him as far as present-day Minnesota, for future publication.

The present book was made possible by the generous cooperation of many individuals; we are grateful to them all. We wish to thank in particular Countess Luisa Sormani Verri Cortesi of Milan for authorizing the publication of her distinguished ancestor's *Giornale*. Also in Milan, Emilio Fortunato at the Archivio di Stato was helpful with the Andreani papers and provided copies of selected documents and letters reproduced here. We also thank Giuseppe Dicorato and the Edizioni Ares for allowing us to reproduce the rare Andreani medal.

We were both studying Andreani's diary independently until Anthony Wonderley, nation historian of the Oneida Indian Nation of New York, told us about our parallel work. His timely intervention prevented a massive duplication of labor (and considerable grief). Others who contributed time, comments, or assistance with this project include Tricia Barbagallo, Neil Blackadder, Marcello Canuto, Rob Cox and the library staff at the American Philosophical Society, Nancy Hagedorn, George Hamell, Kurt Jordan, Constance King, Todd Larson, Frank Lorenz, Tina Meagher, Antonio Pace, Martin Rudwick, Julie Solomon, Valerie Stoker, and Sarah Stuppi. The invaluable contributions of Paul Pohwat, mineral scientist at the National Museum of Natural History, Washington, and Roy Wright (Tekastiaks), peripatetic linguist extraordinaire, are duly acknowledged in the body of the book.

The Department of Romance Languages of the University of Pennsylvania provided a Salvatori Italian Studies Research Grant in 1995 that supported archival research at a crucial early stage. The New York State Historical Association has kindly allowed us to publish parts of Karim M. Tiro, "'This dish is very good': Reflections on an Eighteenth-Century Italian Ethnography of the Iroquois," *New York History* 84 (2003): 409–30.

We also thank our families and close friends, for whom Count Andreani has turned out to be like a guest who never goes home. They have been subjected to the details of his trip to America (and then his trip into print) for much longer than they expected. They have been very understanding, or at least very polite.

C.M.

K.M.T.

Introduction

A Bridge to America:
Count Paolo Andreani and His Journal

Count Paolo Andreani began the journal of his 1790 trip at the northern tip of Manhattan Island. He proceeded to traverse a wooden bridge to reach the present-day Bronx, or, as he put it, "to enter the continent." Travelers of Andreani's day were acutely aware that the city of New York (then confined to the southern end of Manhattan) lay off the coast of North America, separate from the mainland.[1]

Andreani's understanding of geography suggests important differences between his universe—both physical and mental—and our own. He presents us with a long-lost rural world, and he shows it to us from seemingly strange angles. Although he was surrounded by grand vistas, his gaze was often oriented toward rocks and minerals on the ground. His propensity to measure temperature, atmospheric electricity, and even people seems to border on the obsessive. A dog died, he tells us, precisely forty-two minutes after being bitten by a rattlesnake with twenty-nine "knots" in its tail. Even the *absence* of numbers disturbed him: he railed against the therapeutic use of the springs at Saratoga "while there is not a thorough analysis of them of any sort."

Andreani was not alone in his enthusiasm for numbers. His observations reflect the *esprit géométrique*[2] that suffused educated Europe, and the Italian states in particular, in the eighteenth century. Since numbers held out great promise for illuminating the workings of the

1. Of course, culturally speaking, many today continue to hold this view. See Francesco dal Verme, *Seeing America and Its Great Men: The Journal and Letters of Count Francesco dal Verme, 1783–1784,* ed. and trans. Elizabeth Cometti (Charlottesville: University Press of Virginia, 1969), 8; William Strickland, *Journal of a Tour in the United States of America, 1794–1795,* ed. J. E. Strickland (New York: New-York Historical Society, 1971), 89; Jacques Gérard Milbert, *Picturesque Itinerary of the Hudson River,* ed. and trans. Constance D. Sherman (Ridgewood, N.J.: Gregg Press, 1968), v.

2. The term is a contemporary one and has been translated as "quantifying spirit." Tore Frängsmyr, J. L. Heilbron, and Robin E. Rider, *The Quantifying Spirit in the Eighteenth Century* (Berkeley: University of California Press, 1990), 2; Silvana Patriarca, *Numbers and Nationhood: Writing Statistics in Nineteenth-Century Italy* (New York: Cambridge University Press, 1996), 16–17.

natural and social orders, enlightened men and women took to measuring everything from air pressure to population. The United States would catch this fever later in the 1790s, in part through the influence of persons like Andreani. Thomas Jefferson, who shared rock samples with the count, wrote to a colleague that "[t]here is a Count Andriani of Milan here who sais there is a work on the subject of weights and measures published by Frisi of Milan."[3]

Scientific inquiry became the basis of Andreani's relationships with the Founding Fathers, who, like many learned Americans, considered themselves students of the laws of nature. The range of possible topics for discussion may be gleaned from the titles of a series of unpublished scientific studies produced by Andreani in the form of letters. These included "The impact of the sun on various substances," "Brief instructions for capture of butterflies," and "Method for the manufacture of sealing-wax."[4]

The suitability of the travel journal for the purposes of scientific observation enhanced the appeal of travel journals to Andreani and his fellow citizens of the Republic of Letters. In his 1790 journal, Andreani surveyed minerals and rocks he encountered, much as fellow Milanese Luigi Castiglioni had done with American flora.[5] In so doing, Andreani was participating in a controversy over the origin of rocks. Did they owe their composition to volcanic heat, as Nicolas Desmarest and other "Vulcanists" asserted? To a process of slow cooling and consolidation under the crust, as "Plutonists" like James Hutton claimed? Or were they created from water, as "Neptunist" Abraham Werner charged, citing the Great Flood? Andreani fell into the last camp, as suggested by his Wernerian identification of gneiss as a "primitive" rock. His Neptunist sensibilities also were visible in his description of "big boulders . . . most of which were probably transported from far away by the waters of the river, or by some great upheaval" at Manhattan, as well as his reference to "banks" when describing the glacial landscape of the Albany Pine Bush.[6]

3. Patricia Cline Cohen, *A Calculating People: The Spread of Numeracy in Early America* (New York: Routledge, 1999), 112–14, 150–64; Jefferson to David Rittenhouse, June 20, 1790, *The Papers of Thomas Jefferson*, ed. Julian P. Boyd et al. (Princeton, N.J.: Princeton University Press, 1950–), 16:542–43.

4. These were written between 1788 and 1806 but are internally undated. Fondo Sormani-Andreani, Archivio di Stato, Milan, Italy (hereafter FSA-ASMI).

5. *Luigi Castiglioni, Viaggio: Travels in the United States of North America, 1785–87*, trans. and ed. Antonio Pace (Syracuse, N.Y.: Syracuse University Press, 1983).

6. Martin Rudwick, "Minerals, Strata and Fossils," in *Cultures of Natural History*, ed. N. Jardine, J. A. Secord, and E. C. Spary (New York: Cambridge University Press, 1996), 266–86. We are grateful to Paul Powhat for sharing his insights into Andreani's description of the earth.

Although modern historians have paid considerably more attention to eighteenth-century botany than to the nascent discipline of geology during this period, both disciplines were engaged in a global classification project whose goal was to survey natural phenomena in order to expose nature's system. Indeed, the father of binomial taxonomy, the Swede Linnaeus, had proposed an organizational scheme for the mineral kingdom to complement his celebrated botanical one.[7] But rocks and minerals were heavy, and the formations in which they were found were often of greater significance than the samples themselves. Thus, as historian Martin Rudwick has pointed out, geology challenged science's "indoor culture" and promoted fieldwork more than zoology or botany did.[8]

Ethnology also took Europeans outdoors. Because Europeans thought Native Americans were closer to nature, they placed them under natural history's jurisdiction, along with plants, animals, minerals, and the weather. As objects of scientific inquiry, Indian bodies and societies became important to the larger debate over the continent's prospects and limitations, aptly termed the "dispute of the New World."[9] Roughly speaking, one camp was defined by the works of the Count de Buffon, who argued that the American climate limited its natural productions and, by extension, the potency of its inhabitants. The opposing camp was composed of followers of Rousseau. By the time of Andreani's visit, they had been joined by the early American republic's nationalist elite, who were keen to refute the aspersions cast on the continent. Andreani did not fit neatly into either camp, but his observations were conditioned by the agendas and arguments of both.

In addition to its scientific purpose, the journal format retained its function as a guide to advise readers which roads, inns or taverns to seek out—and which to avoid. The inclusion of prosaic details and personal anecdotes imparted to the journal a potent sense of time and place which served to underscore the fact that the writer really *had* been there. After all, it was far from unprecedented for someone

7. Martin Guntau, "Natural History of the Earth," in *Cultures of Natural History*, 212; David R. Oldroyd, *Thinking about the Earth: A History of Ideas in Geology* (Cambridge, Mass.: Harvard University Press, 1996), 193–94. On natural history, see Mary Louise Pratt, *Imperial Eyes: Travel Writing and Transculturation* (New York: Routledge, 1992); Pamela Regis, *Describing Early America: Bartram, Jefferson, Crèvecoeur and the Influence of Natural History* (Philadelphia: University of Pennsylvania Press, 1992); Michel Foucault, *The Order of Things: An Archaeology of the Human Sciences* (New York: Vintage, 1973), 125–65.

8. Rudwick, "Minerals, Strata and Fossils," 270–74.

9. Antonello Gerbi, *The Dispute of the New World: The History of a Polemic* (Pittsburgh, Pa.: University of Pittsburgh Press, 1973); Bernard W. Sheehan, *Seeds of Extinction: Jeffersonian Philanthropy and the American Indian* (New York: Vintage, 1973).

Figure 1. The coat of arms of the Andreani family as revised by Paolo Andreani and registered by city authorities in March 1787. (Courtesy Archivio di Stato di Milano)

to produce a narrative of a place he or she had never visited, a product partly of fantasy, partly of plagiarism.[10] As we will see, there was a bit of both here as well.

"The Dædalus of Italy"

Paolo Andreani was born on May 27, 1763, in the family palace near the famous Duomo, in the city of Milan.[11] Today it is the Palazzo Sormani and the seat of the Biblioteca Comunale Centrale. He was the third male child of Count Giovanni Pietro Paolo Andreani, a prominent nobleman and a senator of that city, and Countess Cecilia Sormani, also of old aristocratic Milanese stock. Paolo Andreani grew up in a Milan where the winds of the Enlightenment and social liberalism and reformism were blowing against the still-entrenched old order. New advances in the fields of science and philosophy fascinated the rising generation of European aristocrats who often struggled to fully understand and embrace the changes that were taking place. Andreani's life and writings reflected the ambiguities and contradictions of his loyalty to his old aristocratic heritage and his sincere interest in the advancement of science and in progressive philosophical theories.

While privileged in social and economic terms, Paolo's infancy and youth were marked by a series of personal tragedies that undoubtedly affected his emotional development and the course of his adult life. His mother died when he was only an infant. In 1772, at nine years of age, he lost his father and the following year his eldest brother, Antonio, who died at age twenty. Thereafter, Paolo's two sisters, Maria Josepha and Daria, left the family palace and entered a monastery. Paolo became the charge of his only remaining brother, the Count Gian Mario, three years his elder, who from that time on acted as his surrogate father.

The family's tragedies did not affect its finances, and the surviving Andreanis, under the able leadership of Gian Mario, retained considerable family wealth. Following the custom of the times, Paolo's first formal education was by a private tutor, and he soon manifested a bright and inquisitive mind. According to Andreani's most recent biographer, at sixteen years of age "cavalier Paolo . . . already enjoyed wide fame for his studies in philosophy, ecclesiastical and secular history, poetry, letters and mathematics."[12] In 1779 he was admitted under

10. Percy G. Adams, *Travelers and Travel Liars, 1660–1800* (Berkeley: University of California Press, 1962).
11. Details of Andreani's early life are drawn from the biography by Giuseppe Dicorato, *Paolo Andreani* (Milan: Edizioni Ares, 2000), 1–34.
12. Ibid., 19.

the pastoral pseudonym of Caridemo Peliaco to the Saggio Collegio d'Arcadia (the Wise College of Arcadia), a highly reputed Italian society of literati who delved into bucolic poetry. The previous year Paolo had entered the College of Modena, a prestigious boarding school for aristocratic Milanese youth. However, it was not long afterward that Andreani began to enjoy his own scientific experiments more than the literary rambles and theoretical dissertations of his professors. Paolo's fascination with the natural world and the hard sciences led him in 1780 and 1781 to ask brother Gian Mario to transfer him from Modena to the famous Royal Academy of Turin, where he wished to pursue his studies of physics, mathematics, astronomy, mineralogy, and science generally, under a more progressive faculty.

For some reason the transfer did not take place. By 1782, approaching his twentieth birthday, he was eager to see the world and continue his experiments independently. Andreani submitted a formal request to Pope Pius VI begging the Holy Father to authorize him to acquire and read historical, literary, philosophical, and scientific treatises and books that had been censored by the Church. He justified his petition on the basis of his eagerness to enrich his knowledge in the various fields of the natural sciences, history, and letters. The request was granted with a few exceptions, including astrology and the works of Machiavelli.[13]

Andreani's first major investment in scientific experimentation bore spectacular results. On March 13, 1784, he astonished a large assembly of family, friends, Milanese authorities, prominent men, and local peasants at his brother's villa in Moncucco, on the city's outskirts, with a successful flight in a hot air balloon. Following a private trial liftoff on February 25 (Figure 2), Andreani's "magic flight" was the first public one of its kind outside France.[14] Inspired by the recent successful flights of the Montgolfiers in France, Andreani had hired a trio of craftsmen—the brothers Agostino, Giuseppe, and Carlo Gerli—to build what the *Gazzetta Enciclopedica di Milano* would describe as a "*Gran Macchina aerostatica*"—a great flying machine. This *macchina volante* carried Andreani and two carpenters who worked for the Gerli brothers to an altitude of about eight hundred meters (twenty-six hundred feet). Owing to the clouds that filled the wintry Milanese sky, the three aeronauts disappeared for some time from the sight of the assembly. The balloon traveled east before landing safely in the countryside about five kilometers away. While the carpenters attended to the balloon, Andreani jumped on a horse and headed back; halfway home,

13. Paolo Andreani to Pope Pius VI, January 15, 1782, FSA-ASMI; Dicorato, *Paolo Andreani*, 27.
14. Dicorato, *Paolo Andreani*, 72.

he was picked up by a carriage and returned to a triumphant welcome at Gian Mario's villa and, later that day, at Milan's opera house La Scala, where he was hailed as the "Dædalus of Italy." The flight was recorded as far away as Philadelphia.[15]

Andreani's flight was more than a flamboyant aristocratic indulgence. It was validated by the scientific ethos of his day. Balloons were regarded as integral to advances in meteorology, which was widely touted as the key to public health and economics. By quite literally broadening the aeronaut's horizons, balloons supplied the new and potentially revolutionary perspectives on the world that had given force to the travel impulse since the Renaissance.[16] If the conspicuousness and daredevilry of the feat attracted wide public attention and acclaim, well, the aeronaut would just have to bear it.

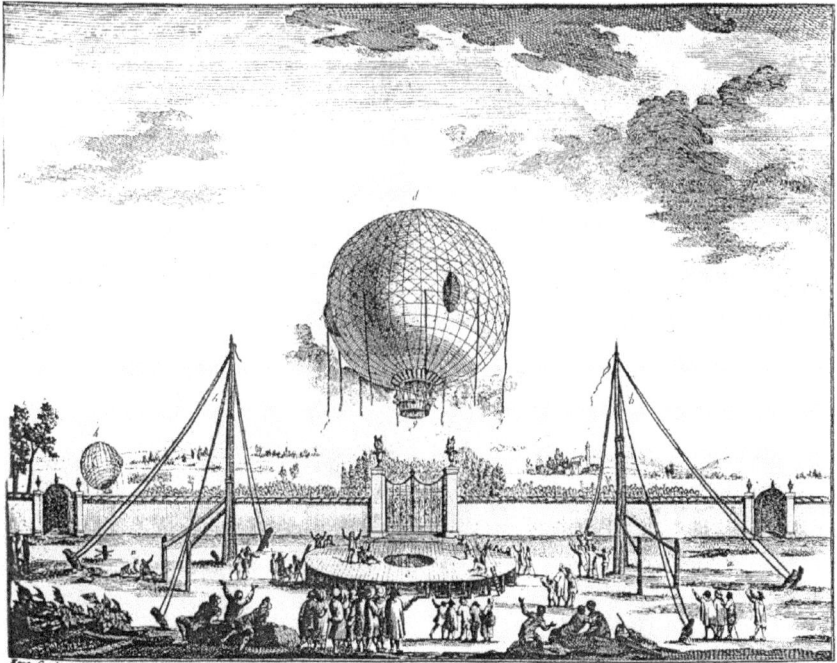

Figure 2. The first balloon flight of Paolo Andreani and the Gerli brothers, February 25, 1784. (Courtesy Archivio di Stato di Milano)

15. *Pennsylvania Gazette*, November 29, 1786.
16. Barbara Miller Stafford, *Voyage into Substance: Art, Science, Nature, and the Illustrated Travel Account, 1760–1840* (Cambridge, Mass.: MIT Press, 1984), 22–24. On meteorology, see Theodore S. Feldman, "Late Enlightenment Meteorology," in Frängsmyr et al., *Quantifying Spirit*, 153–74.

If fame was Andreani's lot, it was nevertheless tinctured by notoriety. In the absence of parental control and domestic obligations and responsibilities, Andreani frequented venues known for gambling and women. His relationship with a certain Signora Chiavacci bordered on the scandalous, and he lost great sums of money at the card tables of Venice.[17] Andreani's gambling was a constant source of vexation for his brother, who more than once had to supplement Paolo's already adequate annuity and even rescue him from near bankruptcy. Thus, when Andreani asked Gian Mario for money to purchase scientific instruments, his elder brother was probably relieved. The staid, sober quality of Andreani's travel journal may have served to reassure at least one of its readers of the author's seriousness and reliability.

It was with this expanded platform of knowledge that Andreani pursued his scientific research, particularly in the fields of mineralogy, geography, and meteorology. Before undertaking his American voyage, Andreani had already journeyed extensively throughout Italy and had visited France, England, Scotland, the Netherlands, Switzerland, and the Habsburg Empire. From 1784 to 1787 he traveled back and forth between Paris, London, Rome, and Naples.[18] In 1784 he visited Scotland with the naturalist James Smithson (after whom the Smithsonian Institution is named) and the noted French geologist Faujas de St. Fond. In 1786 Andreani toured the Mediterranean, visited the islands of Malta and Sicily, and climbed Mount Etna to conduct mineralogical and

Figure 3. A bronze medallion commemorating Andreani's successful balloon flight of March 13, 1784. (Courtesy Giuseppe Dicorato and Edizioni Ares)

17. Dicorato, *Paolo Andreani*, 21, 30.
18. Andreani, *Diario di viaggio, 1784*, ed. Domenico Porzio (Milan: Il Viale, 1975).

atmospheric research.[19] In 1788 he performed a daring ascent of the famed Mont Blanc to conduct similar scientific experiments in the footsteps of the Swiss scientists Jean-André Deluc and Horace-Bénédict de Saussure, both of whom he admired and who had preceded him in that alpine endeavor[20] (Figure 4). That same year he returned to England and this time visited Ireland as well. To the aggravation of his brother and creditors, Andreani's curiosity frequently outpaced his finances. Nevertheless, his gaze was already directed toward America.

"The bearer of the present letter"

As was customary, before departing from Europe, Andreani obtained numerous letters of introduction to prominent men of letters, science, and politics in North America. One of the first such notes was drafted in Paris in March 1790 by fellow Italian Filippo Mazzei, a longtime personal friend of both Thomas Jefferson and James Madison. Mazzei reminded Madison that he was "rather scrupulous" about such letters and predicted that Madison would be able to discern the young count's merit on his own. He commended Andreani to Madison's guidance as to "which persons may be more congenial for him to meet, and who may receive reciprocal satisfaction," particularly persons sharing his interest in physics and natural history.[21]

Early in the spring of 1790, Andreani traveled from France to England to make the final arrangements for his departure and here, too, he acquired additional letters. That April, in London, the historian and philosopher Richard Price drafted a note to Ezra Stiles, president of Yale College, in which he described Andreani as "a Nobleman of character and consequence from *Milan* and a friend to liberty whose zeal and curiosity have determined him to visit the United States."[22] Price used the opportunity of the count's travel to ask him to make a personal delivery to Jefferson on his behalf. Andreani conveyed a political pamphlet written by the noted French revolutionary and mathematician the Marquis de Condorcet.

19. Andreani, *In tour aspettando Goethe*, ed. Emilio Fortunato (Milan: Viennepierre, 2004).

20. Andreani, *Giornale di un viaggio, 1788*, ed. Emilio Fortunato (Turin: CDA and Vivalda, 2003); Ezio Vaccari, "Les *Voyages dans les Alpes* et la géologie italienne," in *H-B. de Saussure (1740–1799): Un régard sur la terre*, ed. René Sigrist (Geneva: Editions Georg, 2001), 197–214.

21. Filippo Mazzei to James Madison, March 23, 1790, *The Papers of James Madison*, ed. William T. Hutchinson and William M. E. Rachal et al. (Chicago: University of Chicago Press, 1962–), 13:115.

22. Richard Price to Ezra Stiles, April 2, 1790, Beinecke Library, Yale University, New Haven, Conn.

Figure 4. Horace-Bénédict de Saussure (1740–99). The scientist-explorer is depicted with his hammer, rock and mineral samples, and hygrometer (at far right), against an Alpine backdrop. From a painting by Jean-Pierre St-Ours. (Courtesy of Martin Rudwick)

Andreani also received a letter addressed to George Washington from John Paradise of Oxford University, with whom the Italian shared an interest in linguistics. Paradise, who had studied at the University of Padua, likewise saw fit to use Andreani as a courier. He asked Andreani to personally deliver to Washington "an ode" by Count Vittorio Alfieri. This fulfilled a request from the author himself. Paradise wrote Washington that Andreani was "a nobleman from Milan, highly distinguished by every valuable endowment, and deserving of the honour of being presented to you."[23] Paradise and his American wife, Lucy Ludwell Paradise, lauded Andreani in similar terms in letters to Jefferson. She portrayed Andreani as "a learned amiable Nobleman . . . worthy of every attention" and invited her distinguished countryman to "take the trouble to introduce Count Andriani by letter to our Friends in Virginia &c. &c. &c."[24]

Since Andreani also planned to travel extensively through Canada, he obtained letters from its former governor, the Swiss-born Sir Frederick Haldimand. Haldimand had played a crucial role in the establishment of the Six Nations reserve where the Iroquois Loyalists had settled after the Revolutionary War, and one of his letters was addressed to the Mohawk leader Joseph Brant.[25]

Falmouth to Halifax

Andreani sailed from Falmouth, England, on April 13, 1790, aboard the packet *Duke of Cumberland*. "Wind from the North-Northeast. Dark sky and light winds," he wrote in his separate *Giornale di bordo*, a small logbook of his first transatlantic crossing, in which he recorded mostly latitudes, atmospheric conditions, and occasional encounters with other vessels. The long voyage was uneventful, except on May 16, when the ship encountered a dangerously powerful storm: "at 4pm

23. John Paradise to George Washington, ca. April 2, 1790, *The Papers of George Washington, Presidential Series*, ed. Dorothy Twohig, et al. (Charlottesville: University Press of Virginia, 1987–), 5:304–5. A copy of Alfieri's *Bruto primo, tragedia* with the inscription "To that illustrious and free man, General Washington" is in Washington's extant library. Alfieri was also the author of *America libera* (Kehl: Pierre Beaumarchais, 1784). See Stefania Buccini, *The Americas in Italian Literature and Culture* (University Park: Pennsylvania State University Press, 1997), 126–36.

24. John Paradise to Thomas Jefferson, April 2, 1790; Lucy Ludwell Paradise to Jefferson, April 5, 1790, *Papers of Thomas Jefferson*, 16:294. Also addressed to Jefferson was a letter of March 25 by John Rutledge, Jr., introducing Andreani as a "gentleman of much information"; *Papers of Thomas Jefferson*, 16:266–67.

25. Douglas Brymner, ed., "Private Diary of Gen. Haldimand, 1790," *Report on Canadian Archives* (1889): 272–75. There is no evidence that Andreani and Brant ever met.

lightning, thunder, and seas so rough that the waves reached twice the height of the Main mast. After we lowered all the sails we were ready to cut down the masts, but shortly thereafter the storm ended!"[26] The ship reached the coastal waters of Canada on May 25 and entered the port of Halifax the following morning. That evening, Andreani wrote Gian Mario to inform him of his safe landfall in North America. "We arrived here this morning," he wrote, "always followed by the brisk winds that accompanied us for the forty-four days that our entire voyage lasted."[27] He expressed disappointment that he could not accept an unexpected invitation from British Admiral Richard Hughes to sail with him on the flagship *Adamant* from Halifax north to the Gulf of St. Lawrence and thence upriver to Quebec City. Lacking letters of credit in that region of Canada, Andreani felt he had to decline.

Halifax held one more surprise for Andreani. He informed Gian Mario that five Native chiefs from the southeastern United States had just arrived, on their way to London to petition the crown for protection against the Spanish. Andreani wrote,

I had lunch with them today at the Governor's, and as they speak a little Spanish thus I could converse with them. The portrait they paint of the oppression they suffer is truly frightening. One thousandth of the truth in their story would today reflect on Spain with horror.[28]

We learn from a long letter that Andreani sent to Francisco de Miranda that three of the five were Cherokees. The others were Creeks. They were the delegation led by the American Tory William Augustus Bowles to petition George III for aid against Spanish Florida.[29] Andreani remarked that the threat of a war between England and Spain—a distinct possibility at that moment—might favor the Natives' stated aspirations to free themselves from Spanish control.[30]

Paolo Andreani remained in Halifax a few more days, just long enough to recover from the voyage and record a few observations of the Canadian seaport in his journal.[31] "Halifax has about seven or six thousand souls," he wrote, adding that "the houses, without exception,

26. Andreani, *Giornale di bordo da Falmouth ad Halifax in Nuova Scozia: Rilevamenti climatici* (Milan: Scheiwiller, 1994), 36.

27. Paolo Andreani to Gian Mario Andreani, May 26, 1790, FSA-ASMI.

28. Ibid.

29. William C. Sturtevant, "The Cherokee Frontiers, the French Revolution, and William Augustus Bowles," in *The Cherokee Indian Nation: A Troubled History*, ed. Duane H. King (Knoxville: University of Tennessee Press, 1979), 61–91.

30. Andreani to Francisco de Miranda, July 8, 1790, *Archivo del General Miranda: Viajes: Cartas a Miranda: 1789 a 1808* (Caracas: Sur-America, 1930), 6:57–62.

31. Andreani, *Giornale di bordo*, 47–51.

are built with wood: some not just properly, but with elegance." He noted that "the main streets are wide and well laid out but poorly paved." He reported that fishing was the principal economic activity, and a few hundred vessels, mostly British but some American, were engaged in harvesting the rich stocks of *baccalà*, or cod. In sharp contrast to the bountiful sea was the surrounding land, which was stony and infertile. Andreani observed that Nova Scotians had to import flour, meat, and tea from Boston, which drove up prices. Halifax was otherwise a well-stocked arsenal serving the British fleet in North America, and Andreani closed his brief commentary on the place by praising George III for the generosity he demonstrated toward the American loyalists who sought refuge in Canada: "many of them," he concluded, "have positively gained in abundance."[32] Interestingly, he reversed this assessment when writing Miranda from New York: "When I compare the coast of Nova Scotia with the beautiful surroundings of this city," Andreani wrote in July, "I can only lament the fate of the royalists, who were obliged to emigrate. A wonderful lesson for all who support the ambitious and despotic views of Kings!"[33] Relief from the sea voyage may have given Halifax a particular luster that faded with subsequent experience. Perhaps Andreani had written what he did at the time out of concern that his writings would be seen by a British official. Alternatively, Andreani may also have simply been currying favor with the Venezuelan revolutionary.

New York, Capital of the New Nation

Eager to commence his tour of the United States, Andreani boarded the *Duke of Cumberland* again for New York, where he arrived on June 6. His first month went well enough that he could write Gian Mario, "Here I am among good people who love foreigners, and receive them with hospitality."[34] With Congress in session, the federal government was in full swing. This permitted Andreani to circulate among the nation's political elite, although avoiding doing so in the city of 30,000 might have been a greater feat. Indeed, as a guest at Vandine Ellsworth's boardinghouse on Maiden Lane, he lodged under the same roof as Jefferson and Madison.

However, Andreani had grown weary of life in the capital even as he praised the city and its setting in the letter to his brother. It seems that Miranda had led him to expect an atmosphere of refreshing republican

32. Ibid., 51.
33. Andreani to Miranda, July 8, 1790.
34. Andreani to Gian Mario Andreani, July 7, 1790, FSA-ASMI.

simplicity. Now Andreani informed Miranda that "things have changed since your visit, and have changed rapidly, and . . . not for the better."[35] He was highly critical of the partisan atmosphere and the court that had sprung up around Washington, which "although miserable, I dare say ridiculous, is nonetheless a Court." It was not that Washington had wished it so, Andreani noted as he wrote of "that veneration for him that I will have forever." He likewise praised Alexander Hamilton, Henry Knox, and William Duer as "the best men in the world" for their hospitality. Andreani was particularly impressed by Hamilton, whose plans reflected both "enlightenment" and "justice" in his estimation. But Hamilton was "oppressed by the whole world"—and particularly by Andreani's fellow lodgers, Jefferson and Madison. While Andreani respected Madison as "the most educated man that I have met here," he thought Jefferson exceedingly proud and avowed that the Virginian "brought from Europe everything bad that he saw there." No one, however, was worse than John Adams, whom Andreani described as "the most pompous man that I know and the most selfish." "God prevent that he become president!" Andreani even exclaimed. The disregard was mutual: Adams later wrote that the count had failed to make a good impression, so he "had paid him but little Attention."[36] Since these observations were personal and referred to powerful individuals, Andreani urged Miranda to keep them in confidence. After all, having been in the United States only a short time, he admitted that he "could very well have been mistaken in a hasty judgement."[37] Andreani had good reason to request discretion with regard to the contents of that letter, as he would learn after his trip through New York and Iroquoia.

Andreani expressed a longing to return to his scientific research. He did not resume it for more than a month, until after Congress adjourned, although he did make a trip to New Haven to visit Ezra Stiles, a fellow number lover.[38] One reason for his delay was probably his good fortune in encountering a diplomatic delegation sent out from the Creek Nation. This one was considerably larger than the group he met in Halifax—numbering about thirty—and was led by the mixed blood chief Alexander McGillivray, who was Bowles's rival.[39]

35. Andreani to Miranda, July 8, 1790.
36. Tobias Lear to Washington, April 5, 1791, *Papers of George Washington, Presidential Series*, 8:67.
37. Andreani to Miranda, July 8, 1790.
38. Stiles recorded a visit from Andreani on July 11; see *Literary Diary of Ezra Stiles* (New York: Charles Scribner's Sons, 1901), 1:398; Cohen, *Calculating People*, 110–12.
39. J. Leitch Wright, Jr., "Creek-American Treaty of 1790: Alexander McGillivray and the Diplomacy of the Old Southwest," *Georgia Historical Quarterly* 51 (1967): 379–400.

A treaty between the Creeks and the United States was concluded on August 7 and received the consent of the Senate shortly thereafter. At precisely noon on August 13, the *Pennsylvania Packet* reported, it was "solemnly ratified by the contracting parties, in Federal Hall, in the presence of a large assembly of citizens.—The vice-president of the United States—the great officers of State—his excellency the governor—and of several members of both houses of Congress." Washington signed the treaty, gave a speech, and presented the Creeks with beads and tobacco. After McGillivray gave a speech on behalf of the Creeks, the "shake of peace" took place, with "every one of the Creeks passing this friendly salute with the president" and performing a "song of peace."[40] Andreani struck out for Iroquoia the next day.

Up the "Udson"

As Andreani bumped his way up the Hudson by stage, he described a region on the eve of a radical transformation. The inhabitants of New York State and Iroquoia stood on the threshold of a vast economic and demographic change, but they had not yet crossed it. The world Andreani described hardly existed two decades later. Within that time, Albany's population would triple, and New York City would surpass Philadelphia as the nation's preeminent port.[41]

Andreani's observations acknowledged the state's potential, but also the distance to be traveled before it was realized. In the wake of the Revolution, New York State remained a backwater. The 1790 census put New York's population at 340,120—placing it behind Massachusetts, Pennsylvania, Virginia, and North Carolina. On a practical level, Andreani's description of his journey suggests some of the challenges that farmers and merchants faced in moving their goods to market. Although Andreani described the roads as "by their nature good," maintenance was uneven, and his progress was slowed by mountains, rocks, and mud. In order to find a passable road along the Mohawk River, Andreani had to make multiple crossings which were not always without risk. We see quite clearly why it cost as much to ship goods a few miles inland as it did to ship them across the Atlantic. Andreani's trip from Kingsbridge to Albany took nearly a week—although of course he stopped to chip, fire, and otherwise examine the rocks and minerals along the route. Three to four days

40. *Pennsylvania Packet and Daily Advertiser,* August 18, 1790.
41. David Maldwyn Ellis, *Landlords and Farmers in the Hudson-Mohawk Region, 1790–1850* (Ithaca, N.Y.: Cornell University Press, 1946), 81; Ellis, "Rise of the Empire State, 1790–1820," *New York History* 56 (1975): 5–27.

was a more usual duration, but a day of travel often began around three A.M. and concluded around ten P.M.[42]

Travel by sloop was more comfortable, more expensive, but not necessarily much faster. The weary stage traveler may not have spent much time at the inns along the way, but the enervating quality of carriage travel doubtless magnified their importance. Andreani's principal complaints here were that food was generally lacking and the lodging was substandard: "Unfortunately we found nothing but some milk, and some moldy bread; and a miserable bed." His observation reminds us of the tenuous nature of rural prosperity. Seasonal food shortages and uncertain harvests were common and tempered farmers' commitment to market-oriented production until infrastructure improved, New York City blossomed, and the United States became more tightly wound into international markets.[43]

Such anxieties, and a lingering perception that one family's fortune meant another's famine, informed periodic rioting directed against the large landowners of the Hudson Valley. They also dovetailed with the egalitarian strains of revolutionary ideology.[44] All these elements were present in Andreani's humorous encounter with a German farmer, occasioning one of the few instances in Andreani's diary in which he made room for another's voice. The farmer, upon learning that Andreani's purpose in visiting America was primarily self-fulfillment, muttered, "*Damn rascals of people* [noblemen] . . . who let others work while they have fun." Yet we quickly perceive that Andreani gave the man voice only in order to allow himself the last word. He proceeded to place his finger squarely on the central paradox of the new nation. Andreani observed that backcountry folk felt the "necessity of maintaining an equality of fortune; while they on the other hand purchase slaves that they force to hard labor."

The institution of chattel slavery was much in evidence along Andreani's tour, particularly in Dutch-dominated areas. New York's

---

42. Elise Lathrop, *Early American Inns and Taverns* (New York: Robert M. McBride and Co., 1926), 29; Thomas E. V. Smith, *The City of New York in the Year of Washington's Inauguration, 1789* (Riverside, Conn.: Chatham Press, 1972), 101; Joel Munsell, *Annals of Albany* 4 (1853): 56; Martin Bruegel, "'Time That Can Be Relied Upon': The Evolution of Time Consciousness in the Mid-Hudson Valley, 1790–1860," *Journal of Social History* 28 (1995): 547–64.

43. Martin Bruegel, *Farm, Shop, Landing: The Rise of a Market Society in the Hudson Valley, 1780–1860* (Durham, N.C.: Duke University Press, 2002), especially 16–19.

44. Martin Bruegel, "Unrest: Manorial Society in the Hudson Valley, 1780–1850," *Journal of American History* 82 (1999): 1393–1424; Thomas J. Humphrey, *Land and Liberty: Hudson Valley Riots in the Age of Revolution* (DeKalb: Northern Illinois University Press, 2004), 112–37; Marco Sioli, *Contro i padri fondatori: Petizioni e insurrezioni nell'America post-rivoluzionaria* (Milan: Edizioni Unicopoli, 1998).

slave population in 1790 stood at 21,324, far higher than any of its neighbors. In Ulster County, slaves accounted for fully 10 percent of the population. When Andreani cited the high price of free labor (no less than a *pezzo duro*—or Spanish dollar—a day), he identified the importance of slavery to New York's economy. Because slaves represented such significant assets to New York's small farmers, the Revolution was not sufficient to overturn their status. Indeed, the state legislature did not pass an emancipation statute until 1799, and even then, the process it specified was agonizingly gradual. Andreani stated that the labor and punishment of Northern slaves were harsh. This assessment put him at odds with other European observers of his day, including La Rochefoucauld-Liancourt, Mazzei, and Brissot de Warville. The discrepancy may be partially attributed to the fact that his trip to New York marked Andreani's first personal encounter with a slave society. To the extent that Northern slaveholding appeared benign, it was so only by contrast to the Southern or West Indian varieties. The historian Shane White has documented the violence of the practice of slavery in early national New York, and his findings suggest Andreani's emphasis was not misplaced.[45]

The aggressive egalitarianism of Andreani's host was not exceptional, either.[46] When William Strickland, an Englishman, asked an Irish innkeeper in Albany to hold his horse in 1794, he said the man began "pouring out a volley of oaths; I was damned for an English Aristocrat, and assured that he would not have held a horse for the King of England; that he was a much better man than myself, being a freeman and a republican, while I was but an English Slave."[47] For his part, J. Hector St. John de Crèvecoeur, who lived in the Hudson Valley, noted somewhat ruefully that Americans were apt to forget "that mechanism of subordination . . . and sometimes apt to forget too much."[48] According to the historian Richard Bushman, these years

45. The 1799 statute applied only to slaves born after July 4 of that year, and they were not to be liberated until age twenty-five if female or twenty-eight if male. Shane White, *Somewhat More Independent: The End of Slavery in New York City, 1770–1810* (Athens: University of Georgia Press, 1991), 86–87; Michael E. Groth, "Laboring for Freedom in Dutchess County," in *Mighty Change, Tall Within: Black Identity in the Hudson Valley*, ed. Myra B. Young Armstead (Albany: State University of New York Press, 2003), 58–78.

46. Saul Cornell, "Aristocracy Assailed: The Ideology of Backcountry Anti-Federalism," *Journal of American History* 76 (1990): 1148–72. Edmund S. Morgan has explained the mutually reinforcing relationship between slavery and egalitarianism in his classic *American Slavery—American Freedom: The Ordeal of Colonial Virginia* (New York: W. W. Norton, 1975).

47. William Strickland, *Journal of a Tour in the United States of America, 1794–1795*, ed. J. E. Strickland (New York: New-York Historical Society, 1971), 127.

48. J. Hector St. John de Crèvecoeur, *Letters from an American Farmer* (New York: Fox, Duffield, and Co., 1904), 78–79.

saw the introduction of the use of the word "aristocrat" as an insult.[49] Such attitudes went hand in hand with the rise of "people's men" to political power. While colonial elites like the Schuyler and Van Rensselaer families still possessed considerable political might, they had to make room for their social lessers, such as the governor at the time of Andreani's visit, George Clinton.

Andreani's political views remain muted in his journal, although there was interest in such matters in Italy. On the same day in 1784 that Andreani made his celebrated flight, the Tuscan *Gazzetta Universale* enthused that in the United States "the form of the republican government is wonderfully perfecting itself, in politics as in commerce."[50] Although he commented on economic matters in passing, Andreani limited his political expostulations to his private correspondence—and even here he was selective in what he said to whom—because he assumed the circulation of his letters would be more limited than that of his journal. In any case, in contrast to the French traveler Brissot de Warville, Andreani had not come to study American society and politics but to study nature. And unlike Crèvecoeur or the refugees from the French Revolution, Andreani never considered making America his home, so he never felt invested in its affairs. His attitude toward popular politics can probably best be gauged by his reaction to news of revolutionary events in France. Writing to his brother in the year before he departed for America, he expressed both his dislike for the French mob and his hope that his fellow *Milanesi* would remain happy and tranquil, entertained by performances at La Scala.[51]

Albany

Albany had made a bad impression on many colonial visitors; it was not yet the state capital, and Andreani felt little urge to revise its image. Since Andreani did not consider descriptions of urban life the proper province of a naturalist, he more or less parroted the account published by the New England minister-geographer Jedidiah Morse (who had in turn obtained much of his information by correspondence). Andreani repeated Morse's claim that Albany's residents had a reputation for inhospitality, as well as his complaint about the filthiness of the city's streets.[52] With a few enhancements, Andreani repeated Morse's

49. Richard L. Bushman, "'This New Man': Dependence and Independence, 1776," in *Uprooted Americans: Essays to Honor Oscar Handlin*, ed. Bushman et al. (Boston: Little, Brown, 1979), 90–93.

50. *Gazzetta Universale*, Florence, Italy, March 13, 1784.

51. Andreani to Gian Mario Andreani, August 31, 1789, FSA-ASMI.

52. Jedidiah Morse, *The American Geography, or A View of the Present Situations of the*

condemnation of Dutch tavern culture and marital and funerary rites, all of which involved much drinking.[53]

Andreani was careful to include a disclaimer that in these cases he was relating things he had not seen, but the description "was solemnly confirmed by General Schuyler an inhabitant and a man of culture." He did move beyond Morse to make some observations on matters closer to his heart—and he took care to specify that these observations were his own. Of the public buildings in the city, he made special note of the prison: "When we visited it there were about twenty inmates, the majority for debts. They are badly kept, without any humanity whatsoever. The building structure contributes to aggravate their punishments." Andreani's awareness of the prisons (as opposed to, say, churches) in his travels doubtless owed much to the general Enlightenment interest in penal reform, whose principal exponent, Cesare Beccaria, hailed from Milan and moved in the same circles as his younger compatriot.

Andreani also contributed an extensive discussion of Albany's climate, complete with a table of twenty-two monthly highs and lows of both temperature and humidity. European expansion had renewed learned speculation regarding the relationship between climate and everything from health to culture to government. Reliable and comparable meteorological instruments were of relatively recent invention, and hopes ran high that systematic observation would reveal patterns of high predictive validity. The implications for agriculture were obvious, and climate was a public health concern of the first order. Hippocratic assumptions that air played a central role in health were widely held, as in Andreani's conclusion at Albany that "the great daily variation in the temperature of the climate could influence the physical constitution of individuals if they did not preserve themselves by always wearing stroud."[54]

United States of America (Elizabeth Town: Shepard Kollock, 1789), 258–59. On stereotypes and realities of early Albany, see Stefan Bielinski, "The People of Colonial Albany, 1650–1800: The Profile of a Community," in *Authority and Resistance in Early New York*, ed. William Pencak and Conrad Edick Wright (New York: New-York Historical Society, 1988), 1–26.

53. If Andreani was willing to repeat Morse's national generalizations, he must have felt comfortable enough with Morse's characterization of Italians in the same book as "excel[ling] in complaisant, obliging behaviour to each other, and affability to foreigners; observing a medium between the levity of the French, and the starch'd gravity of the Spaniards." However, they were also "amorous and addicted to criminal indulgences, revengeful, and masters of the art of dissimulation." *American Geography*, 498.

54. Theodore S. Feldman, "Late Enlightenment Meteorology," in Frängsmyr et al., *Quantifying Spirit*, 154–55; Jan Golinski, "Barometers of Change," in *The Sciences in Enlightened Europe*, ed. William Clark, Jan Golinski, and Simon Schaffer (Chicago: University of Chicago Press, 1999), 69–93.

Axes Along the Mohawk

Weather and health were also directly linked to land use: it had been a common assumption that America was more humid because it was a "new" continent, its forests still standing and its land not yet under extensive cultivation. Documenting the trials of settlers clearing land in the Mohawk Valley, Andreani wrote of "the illnesses that are usually caused by the first exhalations of the odors of a virgin soil." Clearing fields was the primary activity in which the thousands of migrants who swarmed to central New York from New England were engaged. Andreani's description shows why, as the historian Alan Taylor has put it, "the Yankees had earned a collective reputation as the most skilled handlers of the axe in America."[55] Trees were felled for houses, for barns, to let sunlight fall on crops, and, ultimately, to clear fields. This was a family project, Andreani explained, "and nothing is more arduous than the workload they have to endure for the first two years." He described trees in excess of 120 feet high being consigned to the flames. Such was the scale of the burning that Jacob Lindley, a Quaker traveling up the Mohawk three years later, commented that he "was much perplexed for miles, with the continued smoke from the fires on shore."[56]

There was, however, one kind of tree the settlers valued standing more than felled. At Fall Hill, Andreani noted that "[i]n these neighborhoods every farmer cultivates a number of *Erables*' called in English *Maple tree.*" He proceeded to devote particular attention to an unusual industry whose expectations could not have been higher, and which would never be fulfilled: maple sugaring.[57] Although Andreani stated that the sugar was collected to satisfy household needs, many hoped it would supplant its cane counterpart and even bring an end to West Indian slavery. While Brissot de Warville proclaimed that Quaker efforts to perfect this product had been successful, Andreani concluded that the new commodity was not competitive in terms of either price or quality.[58]

That the practice of maple sugaring was nevertheless so widespread at the time of Andreani's visit speaks volumes about land speculators'

55. Alan S. Taylor, "The Great Change Begins: Settling the Forest of Central New York," *New York History* 76 (1995): 278.

56. Jacob Lindley, "Jacob Lindley's Account of a Journey to Attend the Indian Treaty . . . at Sandusky, in the year 1793," *Friends' Miscellany* 2 (1832): 62.

57. Alan S. Taylor, *William Cooper's Town: Power and Persuasion on the Frontier of the Early American Republic* (New York: Alfred A. Knopf, 1995), 119–38; J. P. Brissot de Warville, *New Travels in the United States of America 1788*, trans. Mara Soceanu Vamos and Durand Echeverria (Cambridge, Mass.: Harvard University Press, 1964), 246–49.

58. Brissot de Warville, *New Travels*, 255.

enthusiasm for anything that would raise land values, as well as settlers' desperation for anything that would reduce expenses. Indeed, such was the irrational exuberance of maple sugar's boosters that the Philadelphia physician Benjamin Rush asserted, "It has been said, that sugar injures the teeth, but this opinion now has so few advocates, that it does not deserve a serious refutation."[59] Yet the predictions of maple sugar's profitability were discredited as surely as Rush's position on tooth decay. Although maple sugaring did not die out, its highest hopes proved short-lived. Thus, during his brief visit to the Mohawk Valley, Andreani witnessed and recorded a fleeting moment in its economic history.

Whatever maple sugar's limitations, the valley was nevertheless transformed by human activity. When Andreani visited Fort Plain, it was only with difficulty that he could make out the plan of the fortifications that had been in use only three or four years earlier. They had since been taken apart to rebuild the town, which had been largely destroyed during the war.[60] Andreani captured the postwar scene in his observation that "the roads were covered with men, women, livestock and farm tools of the new colonists." While he had acknowledged the progress of cultivation in the Hudson Valley, the dynamism and human presence in his description of the Mohawk Valley presents a contrast that reflected the separate demographic and economic trajectories the two regions would follow right through the Canal Era.

Andreani and the Iroquois

The trajectory of the Iroquois during the late 1780s and 1790s was considerably different; it was a steep descent. Although Andreani described some of the social disorder that attended the dispossession of the Natives, such as alcohol abuse, he seemed generally oblivious to their recent history. In fact, the Oneidas and Onondagas had lost the vast majority of their territories—literally millions of acres—to the state of New York through treaties signed in 1785 and 1788.[61] The missionary to the Oneidas, Samuel Kirkland, who was one of Andreani's principal informants about Iroquois life, may have downplayed these treaties because of the active and controversial role he had

59. Quoted in Taylor, *William Cooper's Town*, 122.
60. Robert B. Roberts, *New York's Forts in the Revolution* (Madison, N.J.: Fairleigh Dickinson University Press, 1980), 386–87.
61. Barbara Graymont, "New York Indian Policy after the Revolution," *New York History* 78 (1997): 374–410; J. David Lehman, "The End of the Iroquois Mystique: The Oneida Land Cession Treaties of the 1780s," *William and Mary Quarterly* 3rd ser. 47 (1990): 523–47.

played in some of them. However, there were enough negative representations of Native cultures in circulation to explain the Iroquois' condition to the count's satisfaction without having to delve too deeply into more direct causes.

In his description of the Oneidas, Tuscaroras, and Onondagas, Andreani generally adhered to the atemporal, impersonal "manners and customs" format that had governed European representations of cultural others since the sixteenth century.[62] Although there were significant continuities between Andreani's description of the Albany Dutch, the Shakers, and the Iroquois, that of the latter was particularly detailed. In fact, Andreani's Iroquois ethnography followed an implicit script. It was no coincidence that he addressed many of the questions Scotsman William Robertson posed when he researched his influential *History of America* (1777). Collecting information by correspondence, Robertson had asked informants in America if the Natives' physical constitutions were

as vigorous and robust as those of the inhabitants of similar climates in the ancient continent? Was the absence of a beard natural to the Indian? Was he defective in animal passions, the passion of love for example? What was his attitude in regard to parental affection or filial duty? What ideas did he have of property? And what conception did he entertain of a future life?[63]

Benjamin Rush, who had met Andreani only days earlier, posed a similar list of questions to McGillivray in New York City.[64] Rush's and Robertson's questions derived from long-standing ethnographic precedent, but the "dispute of the New World" infused particular categories, especially physiological ones, with greater importance. Thus, Andreani's ethnography reflected not just what he happened to see but what he came to see—lactating women and their children, for example. The Dutch naturalist Cornelius De Pauw had asserted that the relatively long period during which Native American children were breast-fed contributed to degeneracy and lack of vigor.[65] Andreani accordingly

62. Karim M. Tiro, "'This dish is very good': Reflections on an Eighteenth-Century Italian Ethnography of the Iroquois," *New York History* 84 (2003): 409–30.

63. R. A. Humphreys, *William Robertson and His "History of America"* (London: The Hispanic and Luso-Brazilian Councils, 1954), 20; Nicholas B. Wainwright, ed., "The Opinions of George Croghan on the American Indian," *Pennsylvania Magazine of History and Biography* 71 (April 1947): 152–59; Gordon Sayre, *Les Sauvages Américains: Representations of Native Americans in French and English Colonial Literature* (Chapel Hill: University of North Carolina Press, 1997), 98–103.

64. George Corner, ed., *The Autobiography of Benjamin Rush, His "Travels Through Life" together with his Commonplace Book for 1789–1813* (Princeton, N.J.: American Philosophical Society and Princeton University Press, 1948), 189.

65. Harry Liebersohn, *Aristocratic Encounters: European Travelers and North American Indians* (New York: Cambridge University Press, 1998), 32.

claimed he "observed a child of twenty-seven months, who was nourished entirely of the mother's milk, and under the appearances of robustness, and of good health, he absolutely could not stand on two feet." Andreani likewise reported that the Oneidas had little body hair, a fact which had been cited as evidence of Native effeminacy.

It should not, however, be inferred that Andreani was in the degenerationists' camp. For example, his observation that "[a]mong themselves in the family they love each other greatly, and their filial love is no less than that which exists among ourselves," refuted the assertion that Natives' lack of vigor even extended to emotion and expression. Andreani never committed himself to one or the other side of the debate and therefore felt less pressure to suppress contrary observations.

That is not to say that he was shy about passing a negative judgment against the Natives, as in the following passage:

Sometimes a simple action that would be everywhere deemed as madness may among the Oneida Indians lead one to be esteemed a chief, f.[or] e.[xample], one who crossing an immense territory arrives in a faraway nation, [and returns] carrying some sign of his arrival there.

Andreani looked in the mirror but apparently failed to recognize his reflection. His own travel asserted his status as a nobleman in European society, where the voyager (and especially the voyager-collector) had become a heroic figure.[66] Where there was consensus among Europeans that Native culture was deficient, Andreani didn't depart from it, as in his comment that "the Oneidas are like all Indians, lovers of laziness." Andreani agreed that Native land use practices were inferior and uncritically repeated the customary condemnation of the "hardest labor in the field," which Native women performed, and contrasted it with the idleness of the men.[67] Nevertheless, Andreani also acknowledged the political and social privileges women enjoyed, so he at least provided the reader with evidence at odds with his conclusions.

Despite the formulaic manner in which Andreani recorded his stay at Oneida, there is an undercurrent of good cheer in his description. He did not hesitate to record the faults and foibles of New York inns and innkeepers but said of the Indians generally (and of Skenandoah, his host at Oneida, in particular) that "it is truly to be admired the

66. Indeed, in late 1791, after circumnavigating Lake Superior, Andreani was inducted into Montreal's elite Beaver Club, whose principal criterion for membership was that the inductee had spent a winter in the Canadian wilderness. Not having met the seasonal requirement, he was granted an honorary membership (*Rules and Regulations of the Beaver Club* [Montreal: W. Gray, 1819]); Liebersohn, *Aristocratic Encounters*, 2; Stafford, *Voyage into Substance*, 22.

67. David D. Smits, "The 'Squaw Drudge': A Prime Index of Savagism," *Ethnohistory* 29 (1982): 281–306.

earnest attention they express on the occasion of the visit of a stranger." Andreani seemed to reciprocate this hospitality with an enthusiasm that went beyond the norm for Europeans. After hearing the Oneidas sing, he wrote rather casually in his journal that "we were in general surprised by . . . the agreeable melody of the singing of the psalms, rendered in their language." Yet the journal kept by missionary Kirkland suggests the praise Andreani gave out in person was much amplified. According to Kirkland, Andreani said he considered "the melody of their musick & fine soft voices" to be "equal to any he ever heard in Italy." When Kirkland related "this high compliment" to participants of an evening singing-meeting, "one of them replied that he thought '*it was too much for Indians*.'"[68] The discrepancy between Andreani's and Kirkland's accounts of the Italian's reaction to Oneida singing may simply be a function of Andreani's laconic writing style. It may also reflect the peculiar combination of humility and boastfulness a missionary required to retain both his holy credibility and his employment. But if the word and phrase list that Andreani compiled is any guide to his comportment, we may conclude that he was indeed an ingratiating guest.

The literary critic Laura Murray has argued recently that word lists such as these "convey the tenor and lineaments of the dealings, disputes, and chit-chat that characterized relations between Aboriginal and white people far away from life in the metropolis or farming settlement."[69] Compared with other such compilations, Andreani's exhibits a disproportionate concern with pleasantries. It stands in sharp contrast to not only the take-me-to-your-leader and which-way-to-the-food terminology famously translated for Captain John Smith but also the standard comparative-linguistic fare served up by the travelers, traders, and missionaries of Andreani's own day. While some of the phrases he supplied were narrowly utilitarian, he apparently wanted to tell the Oneidas, "This dish is very good," "I hope you would not want to trouble yourself," and "I love this country very much." In dealing with people whom he referred to as "semicivilized savages," Andreani needed to say, "I thank you for your civility." He also translated that rare

68. Walter Pilkington, ed., *The Journals of Samuel Kirkland: Eighteenth-Century Missionary to the Iroquois, Government Agent, Father of Hamilton College* (Clinton, N.Y.: Hamilton College, 1980), 202.

69. Laura J. Murray, "Vocabularies of Native American Languages: A Literary and Historical Approach to an Elusive Genre," *American Quarterly* 53 (2001): 592. On the study of language in early America, see Edward G. Gray, *New World Babel: Languages and Nations in Early America* (Princeton, N.J.: Princeton University Press, 1999); Ives Goddard, ed., *Handbook of North American Indians: Languages*, vol. 17 (Washington, D.C.: Smithsonian Institution, 1996).

gem in European vocabularies of Indian languages: "Please." Indeed, Andreani carried his pleasantries to the point of absurdity. Among the phrases useful to this traveler were "I love your daughter," "She is truly beautiful," and "If I were an Indian I would marry her."

Andreani's description of a lacrosse match suggests the historical utility of his reportage, as well as its limits. His comprehension of the nuances of the game was rudimentary at best: describing its object, he made no mention of goals. As he understood it, the players sought "to make a certain number of rounds of a large field" in possession of the ball. Nevertheless, the sketch of a lacrosse stick in the middle of a line of text provides a striking example of the value of his observations (Figure 5). The anthropologist and lacrosse historian Tom Vennum has noted that this drawing is the earliest extant visual image of a lacrosse stick, and one that "should offer no surprises to anyone familiar with early forms of the northeastern hickory stick" (Figure 6).[70] Andreani's description of the crowd is likewise consistent with other reports. He noted that "a great sum" was often staked on the outcome of a game and that when the wagers were high, "then the women are present, and they proceed with horrible yells to incite the party in which they have interest."

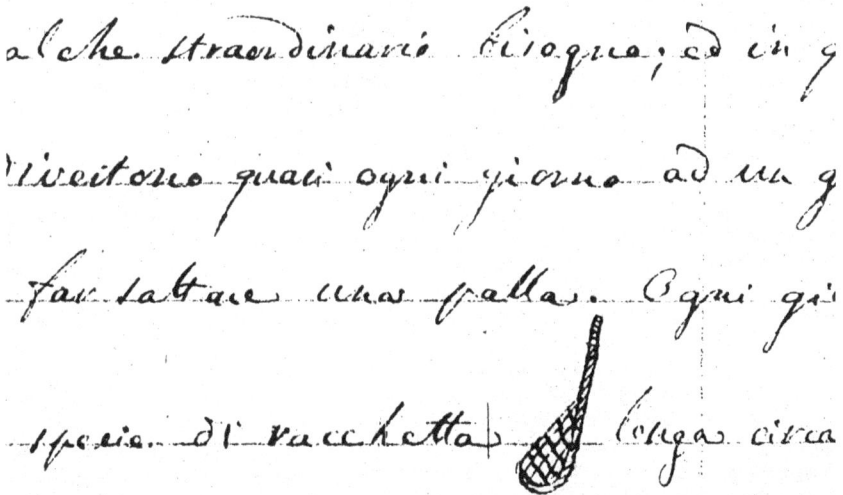

Figure 5. Andreani's drawing of an Oneida lacrosse stick.

70. Thomas Vennum, Jr., "One of a Kind Find," *Lacrosse Magazine* (July/August 1999): 60.

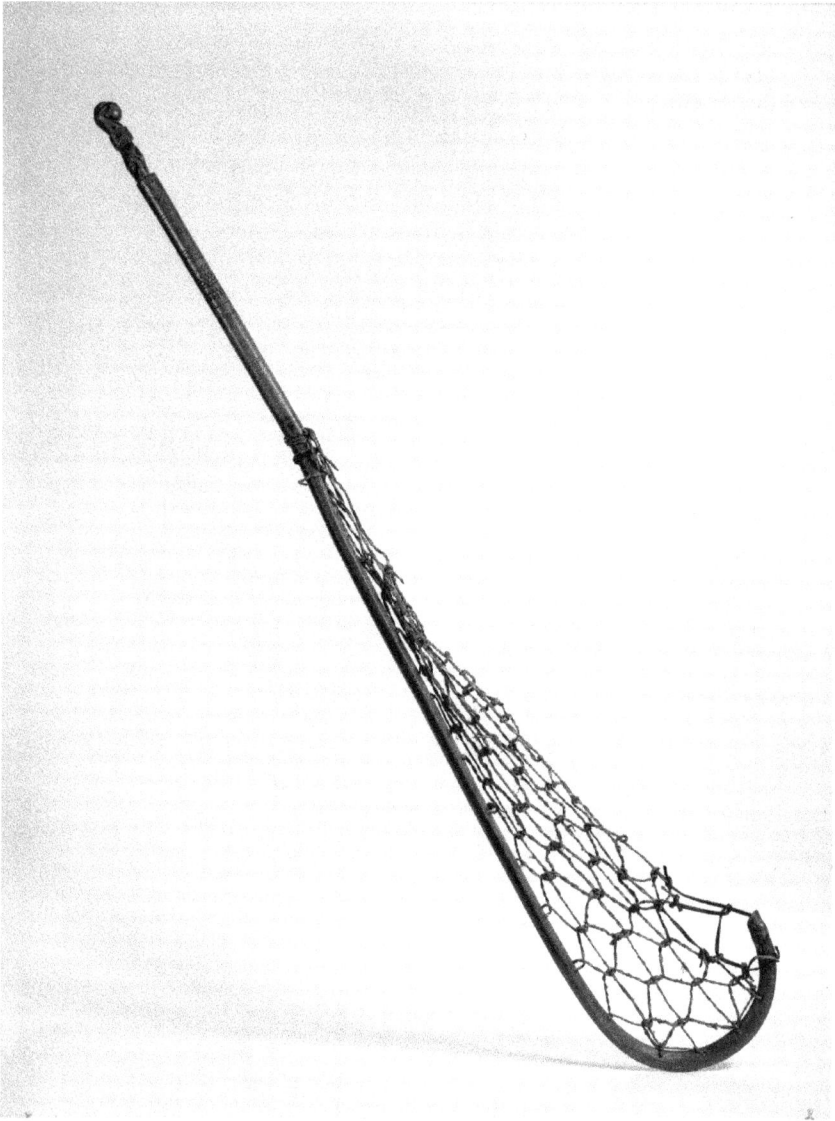

Figure 6. A pre-1845 Cayuga Iroquois lacrosse stick. (Courtesy University of Pennsylvania Museum of Archaeology and Anthropology)

After his twenty-two-page description of the Oneidas, Andreani dispatched the Tuscaroras with a terse paragraph. He wrote, "If we shall say but a few words about this nation, it is because in reality it differs very little from that of which we have spoken, as well for the brief residence we have made among them." And, indeed, he did write "but a few words," mostly about their migration from the Southeast in the early eighteenth century. With regard to the Onondagas, he asserted that that nation "differs little in customs from these other ones, except in the religion." His description ran six pages. What appears to be Andreani's impatience was actually an effect of his taxonomic method. Like some eighteenth-century botanists, he began with a single specimen, described it thoroughly, and described subsequent ones purely in terms of their differences relative to the first.[71] However, the categories of contrast were not pistils and stamens but architecture and communal religious rituals. This approach tended to exaggerate differences along national lines. Although Andreani did not make the point explicitly, the conservatism of the Onondaga nation vis-à-vis the Oneidas was thrown into high relief in his journal.

Andreani's description of the white dog sacrifice reinforces this image. According to Andreani, he did not witness the sacrifice personally because the Onondagas were practicing it exclusively as part the Midwinter ceremonial. Extant descriptions of this ceremony corroborate Andreani's, which stands as the sole documentation of its practice outside the Seneca nation for most of the second half of the eighteenth century. It is doubtful that Andreani received this information from another published source, because his description more closely resembles later ones than those available to him at the time.[72] When a Mohawk prophet at Grand River, Upper Canada, revived the rite in 1798, he was said to have claimed that "the *Upholder of the Skies*" had "made grievous complaints, of the base and ungrateful neglect of the Five Nations (the Senecas excepted) in withholding the homage due to him and the offerings he was wont to receive from their fathers as an acknowledgment for his guardianship." When the revival was exported to Oneida, it ended a thirty-plus-year hiatus for the white dog sacrifice there.[73]

71. Foucault, *The Order of Things*, 142.
72. Tooker, *The Iroquois Ceremonial of Midwinter* (Syracuse, N.Y.: Syracuse University Press, 1970), 102, 114–18, 126–31; Harold Blau, "The Iroquois White Dog Sacrifice: Its Evolution and Symbolism," *Ethnohistory* 11 (1964): 97–119.
73. Tooker, *Iroquois Ceremonial*, 114–18; Pilkington, *Kirkland Journal*, 418.

Generals, Doctors, and Shaker Elders

Although visiting Native communities was one of the principal reasons Andreani traveled to America, he did not consider his visit to New York complete until he examined two other sites of scientific interest, the springs at Saratoga and New Lebanon. He observed that "as a reward for the philosophical [scientific] objects that are lacking on this side [of the river], the traveler walks continuously on historic terrain because this was the field on which the American Troops distinguished themselves for the first time during the last bloody war." Although the search for natural phenomena dictated Andreani's itinerary, he dutifully attended to landscapes of military significance around Saratoga, on Manhattan Island, and at West Point.

While Andreani did not consider his observations on military matters to be "philosophical" in nature, warfare was widely understood to be subject to universal laws discoverable through systematic observation. It was the role of the officer to comprehend and apply these laws. Whereas in previous centuries the aristocracy legitimated its dominance of military institutions on the basis of heroism, virtue, and honor bred by high social station, now education and technical competence played an expanded role. The relationship between science, militarism, and aristocracy was therefore mutually reinforcing.[74] Indeed, while Andreani's balloon flight was an aristocratic conceit with a scientific rationale, the strategic potential of balloons for intelligence gathering and for battle was an early and obvious impetus to their development. And if development of one's military knowledge was not sufficient reason to visit the battlefield, La Rochefoucauld provided another: "If you love the English, are fond of conversing with them, and live with them on terms of familiarity and friendship, it is no bad thing if occasionally you can say to them, '*I have seen Saratoga.*'"[75]

Andreani examined the landscape around Saratoga carefully. Although he did not go into the same level of detail as had the Marquis de Chastellux, Andreani's account is comparable to that of Miranda, who probably encouraged him to visit because, as the Venezuelan put it, "it is so well preserved that any intelligent person can form from it a full picture of the event."[76] As elsewhere, Andreani took particular

---

74. Azar Gat, *The Origins of Military Thought from the Enlightenment to Clausewitz* (Oxford: Clarendon Press, 1989), 28–29, 41; Christopher Duffy, *The Military Experience in the Age of Reason* (London: Routledge and Kegan Paul, 1987), 14–27, 35–43, 50–51.

75. Quoted in William L. Stone, ed., *Visits to the Saratoga Battlegrounds, 1780–1880* (Albany, N.Y.: Munsell, 1895), 100.

76. Stone, ed., *Visits to Saratoga*, 63–87, 100–104; Miranda, *The New Democracy in America: Travels of Francisco de Miranda in the United States, 1783–84*, ed. John S. Ezell, trans. Judson P. Wood (Norman: University of Oklahoma Press, 1963), 100–102.

interest in fortifications and the position of encampments. He partially absolved General John Burgoyne of incompetence and was critical only of the general's failure to seize an opportunity by not pursuing Schuyler after taking Fort Ticonderoga. Nevertheless, Andreani's assessment was that even if Sir Henry Clinton had shown up to relieve his compatriot, the outcome might not have been different.

Andreani conserved his bile for the medical practitioners and self-medicating laypersons at the springs, observing sternly that

many come here to drink them or to take them as bath without knowing what medicine they are applying to themselves, and we ourselves have found various sick people for whom different remedies were necessary. What the result of such carelesness could be is easily understood without any further detail.

His complaints were nothing new. For centuries, physicians and scientists had complained about their lack of control over popular water therapies, and their warnings had been ignored for just as long.[77] In 1783 a Massachusetts doctor who entertained a high opinion of the efficacy of Saratoga water wrote, "It may afford an agreeable amusement to any gentleman of ability and leisure, to prosecute . . . inquiries" into the properties of the waters.[78] Andreani took samples, commented upon the geologic context of the springs, and performed a number of simple experiments to ascertain the water's temperature and composition. However, we have no evidence to suggest that he went on to perform the more detailed analysis considered so important.

From Saratoga, Andreani traveled to New Lebanon Springs, near the Massachusetts border. He performed the same tests on the waters there, which he said tasted less pungent than Saratoga's. Again he took the opportunity to criticize people's willingness to subject themselves to waters of unknown content. However, he kept these comments brief and proceeded to something he found more intriguing yet: the nearby settlement of Shakers.

While the Shakers were accused of diabolism by some of their critics, Andreani's disdain for them did not spring from his own religious scruples. Consistent with the deism of the Republic of Letters, Andreani had remained silent upon matters of religion (with the exception of the beliefs of the Iroquois) until he reached New Lebanon. He

77. David Harley, "'A Sword in a Madman's Hand': Professional Opposition to Popular Consumption in the Waters Literature of Southern England and the Midlands, 1570–1870," in *The Medical History of Waters and Spas*, ed. Roy Porter (London: Wellcome Institute for the History of Medicine, 1990), 48–55; Richard Palmer, "'In this our lightye and learned tyme': Italian Baths in the Era of the Renaissance," in *Medical History*, ed. Porter, 16.

78. Joseph Tenney, quoted in Henry E. Sigerist, "The Early Medical History of Saratoga Springs," *Bulletin of the History of Medicine* 13 (1943): 545.

acknowledged the superiority of Shaker manufactures but regarded their doctrines as incoherent and their form of worship as positively nonsensical. The "extravagance" of Shakerism provoked the journal's most animated chapter. Andreani quoted the inchoate speech of the leader of the religious service he attended and described his strange gesticulations. Andreani's protests that the Shakers were indeed as he described them imply his expectation that his diary would be read by others. To bolster his credibility, he reviewed the sources of his information (manuscripts, interviews with Shaker leaders) and explicitly raised his evidentiary standards. He declined to speculate what went on behind the closed doors of an "*advanced*" Shaker service "because having to rely on the testimony of one who perhaps never entered it, we would be subject to error." He limited his comments to the general service he was allowed to attend. Such a criterion would have precluded his description of the Iroquois white dog ceremonial, as well as the weddings and funerals of the Albany Dutch.

The coupling of practical sophistication and efficiency with "fanaticism" disquieted Andreani. The Shakers' material lives suggested the triumph of rationality; but unreason, rather than being vanquished, turned out to be Shakerism's motivating force. "How," Andreani asked, "can one ever unite . . . customs so excellent to craziness so strange?" In the absence of an answer, he consoled himself that the question would disappear with time: if they adhered to their vow of chastity, he noted, "this absurd and strange sect will be of but brief duration."

Perhaps a tranquil sloop ride back down to New York City helped Andreani digest what he had just seen. That he recorded relatively little of this part of his trip indicates his return was via water, which deprived him of his favorite objects of study. The journal ends abruptly, with Andreani's terse description of West Point. He noted its strategic importance, which had compelled Congress to authorize its purchase from its owner while Andreani had been in New York City.[79] Whereas Miranda found much to inspect and many officers at West Point in 1784, Andreani found the garrison reduced to "twenty men." He commented upon some rocks, but finding himself unable to go farther inland and make more scientific observations, he terminated his journal.

A Different Window

It would be overreaching to claim that Andreani's diary embodied some kind of essential Italian or Milanese sensibility, even if his flattering and

---

79. Alexander Hamilton, "Claim of the Proprietor of West Point, for the Use and Occupation thereof by the United States as a Fortification," June 3, 1790, *American State Papers, Claims* (Washington, D.C.: Gales and Seaton, 1832), 1:19–20.

flirtatious phrase list may invite speculation. Andreani's aristocratic social milieu transcended national boundaries, and the scientific subculture of which he was a part positively flouted them.[80] Nevertheless, like other Italian writers in the eighteenth century, Andreani was less prone to gravitate to either pole of the "dispute of the New World" than his French or English counterparts.[81] Generally speaking, Italian representations of America were less polemical and ideologically driven. The impulse to nostalgically idealize Native Americans or Euro-American subsistence farmers was muted by the fact that even cosmopolitan Milan was underdeveloped by the standards of France or England. Nor was Italy deeply implicated in North American colonialism, either directly or indirectly through emigration or investment. Thus, in Italy the ranks of both America's promoters and opponents remained relatively thin. That is not to say Italian writers like Andreani were more accurate, but the conditions were more auspicious.

Andreani's visit came at a crucial time. His journal of his tour provides snapshots of the expansion and transformation of New York State during a transitional period. He captures aspects of regional development that were nascent, such as the integration of most of Iroquoia into the United States. Other elements, such as the predominance of the Dutch in Albany, were fading but still highly visible markers of the colonial era. Finally, Andreani documented some transformations that were anticipated but unrealized, such as the maple sugar industry. From Andreani's perspective, the transformation of New York into the Empire State appears anything but foreordained.

Of course, Andreani's observations apply beyond New York's borders: much of what he described reflected conditions that existed nationally. His description of the anti-elitism of New York's backcountry population corresponds closely to that of other regions. Castiglioni, traveling in North Carolina a few years earlier, took note of that phenomenon in terms strikingly similar to Andreani's. The plight of Iroquois communities consigned to small reservations was likewise replicated everywhere as the pace of aboriginal dispossession accelerated. Indeed, at the beginning of the twenty-first century we may ponder why some of Andreani's descriptions ultimately resonate not only across the early republic but across two centuries of American history as well.

80. Liebersohn, *Aristocratic Encounters*, 5. When Andreani was elected to membership in the American Philosophical Society in 1792, those inducted at the same time included another Italian, two Frenchmen, one Briton, and five Americans. *Early Proceedings of the American Philosophical Society* (Philadelphia: McCalla and Stavely, 1884), 201.

81. Buccini, *Americas in Italian Literature*, 46.

Remarks on the Text, Translation, and Linguistic Notes

"Tradutori, traditori," or "translators, traitors," goes an old Italian literary proverb, emphasizing that even the best translations ultimately violate the true meaning and spirit of the original. Every *lingua*, both spoken and written, has its idiosyncrasies, its inner meanings that cannot be transferred into another idiom without altering or even losing something of the original in the process. Translations can be even harder when they attempt to reconcile and transfer meaning from an older vernacular, as is the case in the present edition of Andreani's *Giornale*. It has already been pointed out by Italian students of Paolo Andreani that the Milanese count had a quite peculiar writing style.[82] Adding to this was the fact that, like other cities and towns throughout Italy, *don* Paolo's Milan made wide use of a local dialect (known as *meneghino*), to which some Latin was added. Knowledge of "proper" Italian was quite approximate and unnecessary in this prose context, as there was no single standard from state to state before Garibaldi. Written Italian still exhibits considerable variation and freedom of expression of local and social color.

Andreani's *Giornale* reflects such linguistic freedom (relative to earlier and later norms) in a time of revolution. Even today, schoolchildren in Italy, and throughout the English-speaking world, have great difficulty with rules about relative clauses and eschewing double negatives. It behooves a modern editor to translate intelligibly without sermonizing or introducing a level of linguistic rectitude never sought by the author, let alone attained, especially when this style reflects his free spirit.

Andreani's Milanese dialect clearly differs from standard Italian in the use of geminate consonants. On the one hand, written consonant doubling is found in some words with simple consonants, such as his *gellato, dannaro, ferrite*, and perhaps the unclear plural *nubbi*; on the other, standard doubling is omitted where he did not say it, in his *spetacolo, malatie*, and *slite*. In two distinct circumstances, Andreani replaces the modern *i* with the letter *j*, an archaism today: it stands for the semivocalic consonant spelled *y* in English between vowels; and for the vowel *i* at the end of words, especially in plural nouns which could be expected to end in *ii* according to rule, since their singular ends in *io*. Examples from Andreani include: *caldaja* and *ajuto*; *figlj* and *consiglj*.

More original and interesting is PA's (occasional) use of *z* for *s* where

82. Andreani, *Viaggio in Nord America*, ed. Emilio Fortunato (Milan: Scheiwiller, 1994), 12–13.

it has the voiced sound spelled *z* in English and French, which Andreani was familiar with. Thus his apparently ignorant misspellings (of *diverze, sparza,* and *prezentare*) represent recordings of his scientific observation of the phonetic distinction not present in classical Latin, hence ignored in standard Italian orthography today and in his time.

As for proper names and other words which had no standard spelling in English, Andreani writes as he hears, the happy practice of travelers throughout the ages; and happily for us, as it often provides observations as valuable as his notes on minerals and the weather: irreplaceable, even if not of completely modern quality. Even when as trivial as compass directions, these words are kept in Andreani's spelling to give the reader a taste of his style. We have, however, modernized the punctuation where necessary for clarity.

The translation from Italian to English was prepared by Cesare Marino but incorporates various recommendations by Karim Tiro regarding contemporary vocabulary. Translations of Andreani's French letters to Miranda were undertaken collaboratively.

We do not know exactly when Andreani wrote his *Giornale.* He most likely drafted it in its present form upon his return to New York in the late summer of 1790, and even possibly later in the fall, after he resettled in Philadelphia. Since Andreani mentions eating bear meat during his travels to the Great Lakes in 1791, we know that he edited and amended the *Giornale* sometime after that second long trip. However, because the reference to the bear meat was inserted as an interlineated note, rather than interpolated into the original text, we conclude that the temporal integrity of the 1790 diary was retained.

We have converted to footnotes all of Andreani's own notes, which in the original manuscript appear either in the margins or interpolated into the text, as in the previous example. Andreani's notes and ours are differentiated from each other. Andreani's are italicized and identified by special symbols that resemble those in the manuscript and by the notation "[PA's note]," whereas ours are numbered.

It is important to note that this translation has been based in its entirety upon the manuscript. Around 1940, Count Antonio Sormani Verri produced a typescript of the section describing Native peoples that does not always adhere to the manuscript. Some of the inconsistencies present in this typescript were later transferred to the translation by Elisabeth Ruthman under the title "Travels of a Gentleman from Milan, 1790."[83]

83. Elisabeth Ruthman, trans., "Travels of a Gentleman from Milan, 1790," in *In Mohawk Country: Narratives of a Native People,* ed. Dean R. Snow, William Starna, and Charles Gehring (Syracuse, N.Y.: Syracuse University Press, 1996).

In order to avoid encumbering the text with a profusion of footnotes, we have generally limited our intervention to translating foreign and technical terms and identifying individuals and places where they are unclear or little known. Although there are details and interpretations that bear correction or expansion, we have usually refrained from doing so except where clarity requires it. The reader will observe that we have departed from this rule where, in our judgment, the information significantly enhances understanding of or interest in the text.

We have included translations and retranslations of Iroquoian words when they appear significant. These were prepared by Roy Wright, whose initials appear in parentheses in those footnotes. RW's contribution demonstrates quite dramatically the potential of Native-language words as historical sources.

In the phonetic transcriptions that follow, the symbol "7" is a glottal stop and "v" a mid-central nasal vowel. The colon (":") represents vowel length, the semicolon (";") length with accent and the period (".") accent alone. These transcriptions serve the purpose of comparison rather than pronunciation. RW's Oneida transcriptions also appear in Karin Michelson and Mercy Doxtator, *Oneida-English/English-Oneida Dictionary* (Toronto: University of Toronto Press, 2002) unless preceded by an asterisk ("*"). Seneca words are followed by the initials "*WC*" and a number. This indicates the entry in Wallace L. Chafe, *Seneca Morphology and Dictionary* (Washington, D.C.: Smithsonian Institution, 1967).

Journal 1790

Paolo Andreani

[3] From New York to King's Bridge.[1]

=====

14. King's bridge forms the northern extremity of the island of N[ew].
gust York, connected to the continent by means of a wooden bridge which
crosses a river, or more precisely a small sea channel that connects to
the West with the river HUdson,[a] and to the East with the river thus
called.[2] In this location one observes that the flow of the water varies
at every change of the tide, running toward the East when the tide
rises in the River of the North,[3] and vice versa when it is high in the
River of the East. In this location there are two or three houses; and
there are two main roads one leading to Albany, and the other running eastward goes to Boston, and to all the States in the East.[4]

Exiting the City to enter the continent on this side, one takes a road
that runs [4] in the middle of the island, and passably well kept.[5] All
around the city there are a number of hills, which taken all together
form a circular shape. The heights of these hills present nevertheless
some remnants of earthen fortifications, erected by the English army

1. In 1790 the city of New York occupied only the lower part of Manhattan Island.
The King's Bridge, built in 1693, remained the principal artery connecting Manhattan
to the mainland. Although today "Kingsbridge" refers exclusively to the Bronx side, at
the time the toponym referred to the areas around both ends of the bridge.

a *correction 1 amico VB[R?]* [Paolo Andreani's (hereafter PA's) note]. [The "correction" referred to the addition of the H to the phonetic spelling "Udson" that appears
elsewhere in the journal. Other proper nouns are subject to similar irregularities
throughout.]

2. The "sea channel" to which PA refers is the Harlem River.

3. Archaic Dutch term *Noort Rivier* for the Hudson, distinguishing it from the Delaware, or South River (*Zuydt Rivier*).

4. The Albany Post Road; the Boston Post Road.

5. The Bloomingdale and Kingsbridge roads (modern Broadway).

during the last war, and that should have served to defend the city if the peace had not prevented the Americans from besieging it. Their position, and it was their number rather than skill, would have rendered the siege of N. York difficult, and would have offered both sides a brilliant opportunity for their commanders. These fortifications extend all along the entire length for two or more miles past fort Vashington,[6] which is about twelve miles' distance from the City. The position of this fort is interesting, since being situated in the vicinity of the river and on a ground elevated about 45 *tese*[7] over its [water] level it easily guards its course. The English felt the importance of this site sufficiently not to neglect [5] its possession, and in fact they became its owners, capturing the entire garrison. The attack on this fort was conducted with much skill and bravery, and undertaken on three sides at the same time. Since the banks on the side of the river where the fort was built are a vertical drop, they could sail the boats nearby without being easily discovered and this helped a corps of English troops climb on this side.

At the moment that the English took possession of this fort (which today is entirely destroyed) they fortified the high points that one meets advancing from the North, so that they could gain control of the navigation on the river, and consequently secure the communication with the army of General Bourgoigne. The idea was excellent, but the fate and the results were quite different. Borgoigne surrendered with his army to the American forces.[8] [6] The soil of the island of N. York, as we already said elsewhere,[9] cannot be compared in richness to that of the nearby countries. Thus the land is not cultivated except in the vicinity of the few houses that are to be found on the road, which are taverns for the most part. The farmers profit better by cultivating the opposite side of the Jersey, where the soil is fertile. The land fit for cultivation would be of a mediocre quality, if it was not full of big boulders rolled over there, most of which were probably transported

6. Fort Washington controlled the northern access to the island and was situated on a hill overlooking the Hudson. Built in late June 1776, the fort was roughly pentagonal. It was captured by the British in November of the same year. Roberts, *New York's Forts*, 303–7.

7. The *tesa* is an old measure based upon the average opening of both arms of an adult person. The Parisian *tesa* had a universally accepted value of 1.94 meters. Elsewhere in the journal PA also uses British measures.

8. John Burgoyne (1722–92), British major general. PA is referring to the 1777 campaign that resulted in Burgoyne's surrender at Saratoga, which he discusses in some detail below.

9. Although PA probably traveled with his servant, Carlo Pandolfi, his first-person plural is a royal "we"; "elsewhere" most likely refers to another journal no longer extant.

from far away by the waters of the river, or by some great upheaval. We will not speak of any except of those that belong to the soil.

In the vicinity of the city of N. York the naturalist has difficulty distinguishing the rocks that naturally belong to the soil, because besides those that were transported by the causes which we have just pointed out, [7] many are transported daily from distant regions, serving as rock-beds [ballast] for vessels. Nevertheless running on both sides of the two rivers that surround the island, it is to be discovered that the native rocks are of a primitive nature, micaceous leaves[10] with quartz and some portions of clay and of limestone, that is, true Gneiss foliated. This rock varies as greatly in color as in hardness. The iron and the lesser or greater dose of clay cause these differences. At about six miles from the city near the river of the East, this rock is for the most part of a remarkable hardness and of a finer grain. The mica which it contains is of a blackish color, and the vitriolic acid attacks it weakly. Advancing even more, the grains that comprise this rock become smaller, finer, the limestone and the clay [are] in minor quantities, and the color passes to a well-characterized black; [8] and therefore we can give this rock the name of *lorna* as suggested by Mongez.*

The [river] banks at Fort Vashington are foliated, and of the first quality of the rock here above described. Near King's bridge one sees some banks of whitish and friable sandstone. The compound that binds the quartzite parts is limestone.

[King's Bridge to Albany]

12[h].__ Therm. 24°, ___ Hygrom. Saus.[11] 80°__ d° de Luc[12] 42°
         The sky clear with stormy clouds on the horizon

---

10. Semitransparent "leaves," or layers, of mica, a rock-forming mineral. The "leaves" are cleavage flakes of mica, most likely muscovite. Rocks classified as "primitive" were believed to have preceded all others on earth in their formation.
    * *{See Berg. Man. du Miner. article} gneis, and the rock lorne fs. 251.D.* [PA's note]. [PA is referring to Torbern Bergman's *Manuel du minéralogiste, ou, Sciagraphie du règne minérale distribuée d'après l'analyse chimique* (Paris: Cuchet, 1784), translated from the original in Latin and annotated by the French geologist Jean André Mongez.]
    11. Horace-Benédict de Saussure (1740–99), professor of experimental philosophy at Geneva. He invented an instrument that measured atmospheric humidity using a strand of degreased hair.
    12. Jean André Deluc (1727–1817), Swiss scientist. He invented a competing hygrometer

⸻

From the bridge of the king (*King's bridge*) there are not more than 15 miles to arrive to the small village of *Tarry-town*, but in which there is a convenient lodging. Despite all of our diligent efforts, it was not possible for us to pass beyond *Odell*, about three miles on this side. Odell is the name of the owner of an estate of about five hundred [9] acres of land which he possesses in fee simple, and that, following the general custom of the country, provides lodging to the travelers who happen to stop there, and presents them with the bill as if he were an innkeeper by trade.[13] Unfortunately we found nothing but some milk, and some moldy bread; and a miserable bed.

All along these twelve miles the road is mountainous, generally rocky, in certain places dangerous; but on the other hand it dominates one of the more joyous and pleasant prospects we have ever been able to see. The navigation of the Udson river is varied greatly by the sinuousness of its course; but seen from the height of two or three hundred feet, and thus dominating the valleys of the hills that enclose it, the view becomes more picturesque. We visited a number of elevated inlet ridges on the banks of the river, that could be complete delights [10] with little work. The next generation certainly will not fail to take advantage of it.

The rocks of these twelve miles are also of the species of gneiss, and they do not differ except in tint or consistency. It is true that one finds some blocks of a variety of granite, in which the feldspath[14] and the mica abound more than the particles of quartz; but they do not belong to the hills we visited. Following the course of the river, we may be able to ascertain their natural place.

⸻

that used strips of whalebone, not hair. Since he calibrated his instrument in a manner different from Saussure's, the instruments yielded incomparable results, engendering a bitter conflict between the two that was ultimately decided in Saussure's favor. W. E. Knowles Middleton, *Invention of the Meteorological Instruments* (Baltimore, Md.: Johns Hopkins University Press, 1969), 100–110.

13. John Odell's house served briefly as the seat of state government in 1776; in 1781 it served as the comte de Rochambeau's headquarters. Harold Donaldson Eberlein and Cortlandt Van Dyck Hubbard, *Historic Houses of the Hudson Valley* (New York: Bonanza Books, 1942), 16.

14. Feldspar (German *Feldspath*), crystalline minerals consisting of aluminum silicates with either potassium, sodium, calcium, or barium.

5. *d°*. From the place where we spent the night, to the little village of Peek-skill lands, there are in fact only 21 miles to journey, but it is such a road, that instead of advancing, the horses were barely able to get us there. From place to place there are some tracts of passable [road], and here and there it is so ruinous that one would take a great risk in getting on it during the night-time.

[*11*] At 9 miles from the place where we lodged at night there was a silver mine that had been worked on in times past. The quarry is at the base of a small elevation, and right at the level of the Hudson river. The owner of the estate, a certain Hunter, accorded its exploitation to a company of associates in exchange for 10 p% of the profits. The mine produced more than what one would have expected given the inexperience of its foremen.[15] The war suspended the work for some time; and because today some quantity of water has entered the tunnels, the work has been entirely suspended. I have seen some nice pieces of native silver that were extracted from this mine.

At this site the river Hudson is of a much greater width, because at about a ½ a mile it receives the waters of the Croton river, which has its spring about fifty miles [*12*] away to the E.N.E. At about three miles' distance one crosses this river on a boat that serves as transport (Ferry), and it is at this point about sixty *tese* wide, of little depth, of a smooth course, and of a constant mass of water. The tide enters it, but because its bottom is full of stones, it cannot be navigated.

A few miles farther ahead, exiting a few hundred paces from the road, one enjoys one of the most cheerful views of the Hudson river that it presents all along its [entire] course. Here it resembles more a lake than a river, and the mountains that surround it on the opposite western bank rise gradually in a nice and imposing shape.

Peek's Kill Lands is a small village distant about a ½ m^a [mile] from the river, and there is a passable lodging kept by a certain Birdsall.[16] This place serves as a wharf for loading the products of the factories[17] in the interior on boats, [*13*] and here small boats are built as well.

15. The mine was worked by an English company until the Revolutionary War. The owner of the estate was Elijah Hunter; its prewar operations were directed by one Colonel James. J. Thomas Scharf, *History of Westchester County, New York* (Philadelphia, Pa.: L. E. Preston, 1886), 2:323–25.

16. Daniel W. Birdsall (1735–1800) was the owner of an inn that boasted George Washington among its distinguished guests. While PA regarded it *passabile*, James Madison, in his "Notes on Hudson Valley Lodging," rated the inn "excellent." George A. Birdsall, *The Birdsall Family: Genealogy and History* (Annandale, Va.: n.p., 1958); James Madison, "Notes on Hudson Valley Lodging," [April 24, 1791], *Papers of James Madison*, 14:14; Scharf, *History of Westchester*, 375, 391.

17. Trading posts.

Along this road we have observed that the population diminishes sensibly, and one only finds houses more rarely.

The ground is more mountainous, more full of stones, and more covered with original virgin forests. Some of the houses resemble very much Irish huts. They are built of logs placed on top of each other; and the cracks are filled with kneaded mud of a cretaceous nature. The weather having been raining during the entire day we could not visit the surrounding hills.

———

16. d°. From Peekskill = Lands we advanced in this day an additional twenty miles, until the village of *Fish*==kill. Along this stretch it is solitude almost everywhere, and the road is opened in the middle of narrow valleys and across hills, and is so badly kept that [*14*] it is possible to advance only at a slow pace. The few homes that one finds are of the ultimate shabbiness. Since the ground is elevated, it bears the name of High=lands.

In the few moments that the rain stopped we viewed the surrounding hills to locate the natural place of the boulders of granite that are found on the road; but our researches were in vain. They are for the

Figure 7. Entrance to the Highlands near Fishkill, drawn by William Strickland, 1794. (Courtesy New-York Historical Society)

most part composed of gneiss; and others of foliated clay, of reddish color. The ancient vegetation is otherwise a great obstacle to the investigation of the ground.

Ahead of arriving at the village, one enters a valley of an oval shape surrounded by little hills. Here the scene changes completely; and one passes rapidly from a deserted place to a garden. The soil is richer, well cultivated, and there are habitations at every step. Fish-kill is in the center of the valley, and it is composed of about thirty good houses. There are two churches, and almost all the inhabitants begin [15] to speak Dutch. A certain Van Wyck there runs a true inn,[18] but in the summer it is entirely lacking provisions. The eight months of the good season the majority of the passengers travel by water, and there is no transit by land except during the time of the ice that closes the navigation on the Udson.

=====

'. d°. At 14 miles from this last village there is a town with a Judicial seat called Poughkeepsie, and the road runs always along a fertile country, well populated and by appearances rich. The naturalist has nothing to examine. The hills are left behind at the distance of a few miles, and the land is covered with several feet of vegetable soil. At four miles I was taken to examine a *curious* spring and we were fooled in our expectations. All the curiosity is reduced to [16] having the waters clear and at times more abundant, without still any shadow of periodicity.[19] We were also taken to observe the beginnings of a mine about six miles away; and instead of metal we found banks of slate of a greenish color containing big cubes of pyrite.[20]

The Town has about eighty houses some of which are properly built, and two churches. The prisons are new, properly kept. I found but three prisoners.[21]

=====

18. Isaac Van Wyck, who was one of the three partners holding the exclusive right to operate the stage between Albany and New York. Joel Munsell, *The Annals of Albany* 4 (1853): 56; Helen Wilkinson Reynolds, *Dutch Houses in the Hudson Valley before 1776* (New York: Payson and Clarke, 1929), 66.

19. Disappointed, PA asked James Madison for information about it. Madison appended a note to his aforementioned list of inns, "*near this a curious spring noted by Colles in his chart enquire of it for Ct. Andriani.*"

20. Fool's gold.

21. There was a single prison, which shared a roof with the courthouse and the tavern. Alden Chester, *Courts and Lawyers of New York* (New York: American Historical Association, 1925), 3:1310.

18. *d°.* This day we crossed a country well cultivated, without however having a place to make any observations; and along the way we found several new settlements. In the evening we took lodging in the village of Red=Hook in a passable tavern kept by Giacomo Svartz.[22] This village is at a distance of twenty-five miles from Pough-keepsie.

=====

[*17*]

19.*d°.* The pouring rains of the last two days so ruined the roads, which are by their nature good, that we were not able to arrive at Kender=hook as we had originally planned. After 24 miles we stopped at a tavern kept by a *fermiere* (farmer) about six miles from the village. The house is good, but we found it lacking in every thing.

=====

20.*d°.* Along the 26. miles that there are to get to Albany, from the place where we spent the night, the population is larger, and one finds new dwellings at every step.

The road is also very good, but the taverns are usually detestable. At every place where a stranger stops, the host, before offering anything, starts by tormenting him with a thousand questions, for no reason other than curiosity. Name, country, profession &c and such questions are the first. Afterward follow others [*18*] more varied on the country, on the customs, and it ends with the praise of America. We had fun at their expense, posing now as wheat merchants, now as doctors &c and we were always believed. Only one time we told the truth, and we were regarded as impostors. Where do you come from? from Italy. Is it possible? said the host; and then turning toward his wife he added in bad German: listen, they come all the way from Italy to seek fortune upon us. What is your job, and for what reason do you come? Are you perhaps directed to settle in the interior lands (in the back country)?

No, I am a nobleman, I eat my annuities, and I travel only to have fun, while others work for me. *Damn rascals of people* who are these who let others work while they have fun. I have heard, he continued, that there are in *Francia vecchia* (in the old France) some of these, but thank God we do not have them here, [*19*] and if our children will not lose their brains, they will prevent such people from developing. Such is the idea held by the inhabitants of the interior country of the

22. Presumably Jacobus Swartwout. Madison rated this inn "very good."

necessity of maintaining an equality of fortune; while they on the other hand purchase slaves that they force to hard labor, and they have them put in prison at the smallest suspicion of escape. My man was at the same time colonel and Cincinnatus.[23]

The hills that overlook the road are of varied nature, and some of them are of limestone, containing pieces of petrified shells. Before arriving in Albany one must cross the river on a boat, the city being built on the western banks. From far away it seems much more impressive than what it is in reality.

[20]   Of the City of Albany.

═══

This city is one of the oldest in its origins of all in North America, since it was erected in municipality (*incorporated*) in 1686* shortly after the discovery of the Hudson river. It is situated on the western banks of this river 160 miles north of New York under the degree 42° 36' of northern latitude.[†]

The soil of its neighborhood is by its nature fertile for some products, for ex. corn and good pastures, and the inhabitants have contributed to it not a little with their work to render it ever more fertile. On both sides of the river there is a continuous series of farms, and there are few patches of land left uncultivated; and these because they are of a much inferior condition.

The site of this city was selected with [21] considerable cleverness, being naturally situated in a place of commerce; the river being navigable up to under its walls by boats of eighty tons, and communicating by water with the interior factories both to the North, by the Hudson itself, and to the West by the Mohawks river, both navigable to their

---

23. A dictator and an egalitarian. After his victory in 458 B.C.E. on the Equii, Lucius Quinctius Cincinnatus gave up his dictatorship and returned to the simple life of a farmer. His example was widely hailed in the early American republic. Although PA did not have a copy of Luigi Castiglioni's *Viaggio* in 1790, Castiglioni made a very similar comment concerning the inhabitants of the North Carolina backcountry: "if a traveler in answering their questions reveals that he is not a merchant, or a doctor, or that he does not intend to settle in America, they look upon him suspiciously, thinking it is impossible that one might travel solely to educate himself." Castiglioni, *Viaggio*, ed. and trans. Pace, 180.

* *Smith History* [PA's note]. [PA is referring to William Smith, *History of the Province of New York*, originally published in 1757.]

† *V. Morse Geog. pag. 298.* [PA's note]. [PA's description of Albany owes heavily to Jedidiah Morse's *American Geography*, 244, 258–59.]

headwaters by flat boats, and thence with a few miles of transport over land communicating with lakes of an immense surface. The river Mohowks joins the Udson about seven miles distant from Albany, and it is said that it has its spring a few miles north of Fort Stanwix:[24] but as we shall have place farther below to speak of it in greater detail, thus we shall not express our doubts here.

The Northern River is commonly believed to take its origins toward the 44° of latitude in an area enclosed by the two lakes Ontario and Champlain, but we are informed by a person of great accuracy in his observations, and who himself has made various trips to those places, [22] that the position assigned in the geographical charts is completely wrong. He suggests that [the river] descends from some mountains that surround the southern part of the South Western branch of the St. Lawrence river, commonly known in the maps with the name of *Cadarakui* river.[25]

At the present time the commerce of this city consists only of the export of products of the soil, and of the import of all the other items of daily consumption, and of luxury items. Among the different kinds of grain, wheat and oats are the first articles exported, and both are of excellent quality. The wood for construction, both for maritime use in the shipyards, and to build homes, is also respectable. But on the other hand the imports are noticeable because in the entire city, and in its surroundings, there is not a single factory of any consideration; except for a mill not yet completed, for the [23] preparation of Virginia tobacco, and for grinding cocoa and mustard; which will employ about 40 people, and will serve the needs of the town.[26]

There was some time earlier a glass manufactory which went broke through the poor conduct of the managers.[27] The lack of manufactures has to be attributed more to the costs of manpower than to the inactivity

24. This fort protected the Oneida Carrying Place, a strategic portage between the Mohawk River and Wood Creek in present-day Rome, New York. It was also known as Fort Schuyler.

25. Cataraqui River. Cataraqui was the aboriginal name of Kingston, on the northern shore of Lake Ontario. The name Cataraqui appears on John Mitchell's 1755 "Map of the British and French Dominions in North America," which PA probably consulted in the 1775 edition titled "A Map of the British Colonies in North America."

26. Caldwell's Mills. That they had commenced operations in March suggests PA did not see them personally. Tricia A. Barbagallo, "James Caldwell, Immigrant Entrepreneur," *Hudson Valley Regional Review* 19 (2000): 55–68.

27. The Dowesborough Glass House was struggling but still in existence. In 1789 its owners petitioned the state for a grant, citing the difficulty of competing with the glassworks subsidized by Massachusetts. The legislature of New York accordingly appropriated £1500. Susan E. Lyman, "The Albany Glass Works and Some of Their Records," *New-York Historical Society Quarterly* 26 (1942): 55–61; Hamilton Manufacturing Company Papers, New-York Historical Society.

of the inhabitants: A carpenter or bricklayer cannot be employed at less than a *pezzo duro*[28] a day. In the interior parts the price varies by about one eighth; but a daily farmhand costs half a *pezzo duro* plus his meal.

The inhabitants of Albany are about 4,500 in number and are the majority of Dutch extraction; and they commonly speak that language. Nonetheless today few are the families that have preserved intact their origin, that did not subsequently mix with the new adventurers, coming principally from Ireland and Scotland. It is possible that at the time of the [*24*] establishment of this community, the founders brought with them the scrupulous neatness that one observes in the homes in Holland and in its streets: but today it is all the opposite. The streets are muddy in the warmest days of the summer and the few ones one finds paved, they are so unworthily.

The interiors of the homes correspond to their old heavy and rough exterior, except for a few new homes. The public buildings are for the most part old and decayed. There are various churches and a Town-house[29] and a prison. When we visited it there were about twenty inmates, the majority for debts. They are badly kept, without any humanity whatsoever. The building structure contributes to aggravate their punishments: but we observed the beginning of a new building for this use, which progresses extremely slowly.

In the entire city there is not a single hospital: a great inconvenience anywhere, especially where the doctors charge [*25*] a great fee. The true poor find it impossible to have access to the [medical] art, which is therefore in itself useless.

The inhabitants of this city have the shameless reputation of not cultivating hospitality, and of not conversing with strangers, or to put it better, with the new residents. The reason for this latter reputation is easily found in the jealousy which must naturally emerge among few individuals, who living on a small limited area compete to steal from each other the commissions and the opportunities for earning.[30] As for ourselves, we can state little regarding these two matters, our stay having been too short to be able to express a sound judgment. That which has appeared to us is that there is more dissipation mostly among the

28. The Spanish *peso duro* of 8 silver *reales,* also known as the Spanish dollar. At the time, it was worth about 8 shillings and 5.6 Italian *lire.* The dollar was not adopted by the United States until 1792.

29. Town Hall.

30. Morse wrote: "A heterogeneous collection of people, invested with all their national prejudices, eager in the pursuit of gain, and jealous of a rivalship, cannot expect to enjoy the pleasures of social intercourse or the sweets of an intimate and refined friendship." *American Geography,* 258–59.

youth, who from morning until evening gather in the billiard rooms, or sit in a coffee house with a pipe in their mouth without speaking or speaking badly as there is no culture of the spirit of any sort.

[26] Before arriving in this city we were informed of some curious practices that are observed nevertheless in marriages and in funerals; and even though we did not have the opportunity to witness them ourselves, nonetheless that which we shall add was solemnly confirmed by General Schuyler[31] an inhabitant and a man of culture.

The original Dutch when they marry, which is usually among themselves, do not celebrate the nuptial formalities as elsewhere in the presence of relatives and with a sumptuous banquet the same day; but to this they attend at the eleventh hour of the day following the nuptials; the groom is expected to receive all of his friends without any sort of invitation, and the rooms are full of tables with a cold buffet and wine in abundance.

As they enter their seats without any sort of compliment adapted to the occasion, and no one can get up, or to put it better, no one likes to get up [27] before [they achieve] a general drunkenness, revolting to human nature.—

In the funerals there is something yet more repulsive. The day the corpse has to be delivered to the tomb, the closest relative of the deceased circulates an invitation to all the relatives and friends to convene at the house at a given hour. Some of them are responsible for carrying the coffin, and others follow them in a procession. After having completed this sacred function the group gathers at the home of the deceased where the heir entertains it with tobacco and wine. If the deceased was a man of reputation and generally loved, the group abstains from extravagance: but in the case in which he is of doubtful fame, the most rightful ceremony is turned into a spectacle, and above all in the case of a stingy one, songs are even sung to express the good that has resulted with his death. [28]

We shall close this subject with a few words on the climate. The city of Albany suffers a more intense cold in the winter than N. York, even greater when one compares the difference in latitude; and a few days of the summer the heat is likewise more sensible because it does not partake of the cool [breeze] of the sea and of the confluence of the

---

31. Philip John Schuyler (1733–1804), American general during the Revolutionary War. PA bore a letter of introduction to him from his son-in-law, Alexander Hamilton. In turn, Schuyler gave PA a letter to Samuel Kirkland, the missionary to the Oneidas. *Papers of Alexander Hamilton*, ed. Harold C. Syrett (New York: Columbia University Press, 1962), 6:552.

two rivers like in this latter city. The maximum cold observed was –26°
of Reaumur,[32] and the maximum warmth of +24.5°. But that which
renders the climate disagreeable, especially to a foreigner, are the
daily changes that occur in the city. The following example will illustrate this. The day 22 of August of this very same year (1790) at 6. A.M.
the sky was clear bright, the wind E.S.E. the thermometer +24.3°; at
5. P.M. the sky clear, the wind having shifted to N.E. the therm. found
itself to be +15.2°. There was therefore a variation of nine degrees
and a decimal in the space of a few hours; and I was assured that
such a variation is at times much more sensible. [29] During my stay
I did not fail to examine the status of the atmospheric electricity, but
I did not have any sign except one time only and this quite weak, even
though the electrometer was armed with a conductor and elevated
circa eight feet above ground. The humidity of the air must be great,
since during four days of continuous clear [sky] the inhabitants
were pleased with the dryness of the air, while the hygrometer of Saussure was maintaining with little variation at 86° and that of de' Luc at
45°. ——

The river Udson is usually frozen at the beginning of December,
some years in November as well, and the navigation is not free of the
great ice blocks until March [is] advanced. During all this time the
ground is covered by several feet of snow; and the inhabitants take
advantage of this circumstance to transport the goods on the sleds
from the interior parts to the different loading sites.

The great daily variation in temperature could influence the physical constitution of individuals [30] if they did not protect themselves
by always wearing stroud.[33] The greater variation of the Barometer in
the space of 24 months was of 3 inches and 1 line, English measure,
as it will be easier to see in the table herein annexed of some Baro-
metric and Thermometric observations kept by the Secretary of a
[Scientific] Club. We did nothing but extract the maximum and the
minimum of every month, and to convert the English measures[34] into
the French ones.[35]

———

32. René-Antoine Ferchault de Réaumur (1683–1757) invented an alcohol thermometer in 1734.
33. An inexpensive trade cloth imported for Indian blanketing.
34. The Fahrenheit scale introduced in 1714.
35. The centigrade scale introduced in 1742.

		Barometer		Thermometer	
		Maximum	Minimum	Maximum	Minimum
Year 1788	April	28,6,1	28,3,0	+12,5°	+2,6°
	May	28,4,0	27,1,3	22,2°	8,7°
	June	28,3,1	27,5,6	25,6°	10,5°
	July	28,1,6	27,7,9	25,6°	14,7°
	August	28,5,2	27,11,4	23,0°	13,7°
	September	28,3,5	27,9,1	19,9°	8,5°
	October	28,7,7	27,7,0	13,4°	−4,6°
	November	28,7,3	27,5,6	14,2°	2,4°
	December	29,1,2	27,7,9	+6,8°	−13,9°
Year 1789	January	28,5,1	27,7,9	1,8°	11,3°
	February	28,8,4	27,8,3	3,5°	25,1°
	March	29,1,2	27,7,9	6,4°	6,4°
	April	28,5,1	27,2,5	16,0°	0,5°
	May	29,1,2	27,2,6	18,6°	+4,0°
	June	29,1,2	26,3,1	19,4°	9,0°
	July	29,1,3	27,7,9	20,6°	10,7°
	August	29,1,2	27,8,3	26,3°	11,8°
	September	28,7,3	27,8,3	16,8°	8,2°
	October	28,3,0	27,8,3	10,7°	0,9°
	November	28,9,5	27,7,9	9,8°	−3,9°
	December	28,8,2	27,6,8	5,6°	9,0°
1790	January	28,7,4	27,8,1	2,4°	10,5°

[32]   From Albany to the Six Nations

════

24. d°. The most passable road from this city to the country inhabited by the
Indians of the Six confederate Nations is along the river Mohocks,
which, as we have noted earlier, unites with the Udson at a few miles'
distance from Albany. The first village of significance that is found on
this road is that of Schenectady, which lies on the banks of this first
river, seventeen miles distant from the city. This journey is truly dreary
for travelers and tiring to the horses, to these [the horses] for the reason of the dusty, cretaceous nature of the terrain, and for those [the
travelers], because they pass through continuous uninhabited woods,
and a soil monotonous almost always flat.[36] Now and then one sees
some slightly elevated banks, composed they too entirely of sand, and

36. PA is passing through the Albany Pine Bush along the King's Road.

the few rocks that one encounters now and then scattered [*33*] on the ground are of their nature rolled, and perhaps are there only by chance. This village is inhabited almost entirely by Dutch families, is passably built, and the roads are spacious and almost all at right angles. Before the last war this village did a respectable business with Canada'; but since the English provinces can no longer trade with the Foreign States, Schenectady has suffered greatly, and we [no] longer find present [anything other] than the *entrepôt* of the goods and products of the interior parts of the State of N. York, which come down until here on the river Mohocks, and pass afterward on wagons to Albany; because a few miles before the confluence of this river with the Udson it falls from a height of about seventy-two feet.[37] There is a road on both sides of this river, but because that on the northern side is considered the best, that is, not the worst, thus we crossed the river under the walls of the village, not to abandon it [*34*] any more except now and then for brief moments. The location of the village of Schenectady is picturesque, and generally all along this river, from its

contain.

A STAGE COACH OF THE LAST CENTURY.

The Western Mail Stages from Albany to White town and Cooperstown.

Figure 8. An eighteenth-century stagecoach. From Joel Munsell, *Annals of Albany*, vol. 4 (Albany, N.Y.: Joel Munsell, 1853).

37. Cohoes Falls.

spring North West of Fort Stanvix to its confluence with the Northern, its banks are pleasantly varied, and the hills which on both sides border its course, are covered with leafy woods, interspersed from time to time by cultivated fields and by pleasant prairies. The first twelve miles of way, which thus many are counted to the tavern of Grotts[38] in which we lodged at night, pass through a sequence of lands almost all cultivated, and often one encounters the dwellings of *fermieri*/farmers; following the custom of the country almost all of them keep *osteria* [lodging].

The hills that overlook the road are almost all made of a rock of blackish flint, with a fine and tight grain that produces sparks when hit with a piece of steel, and others of a granitic rock. This granite is almost always [*35*] composed of four substances, quartz, feld-spath, schorl, and a greenish mica, not in fact mixed among themselves, but divided one from the other in the form of very thin veins. The feld-spath seems to be the overabundant component in some pieces, and it is of a reddish color: in others, mica dominates. In between these hills of granitic rock and of *lorna*, we observed some banks of a blackish clay, hard, leafy.

At thirteen miles' distance from the inn of Grotts there is the little
25 *d°.* village of Tripps=hill[39] situated pleasantly up on a plain elevated about three hundred feet from the sea level from which it is not removed [more] than a few hundred paces. This elevated position is far more preferable to place dwellings, to remove them in such a way from the damage suffered by those that are built on the plains near the river, which exits its bed almost twice annually, flooding all the nearby country. These water expansions [*36*] serve in general to improve the lands, because since the river does not carry with it either stones or sand, but only deposits muddy soil that we found to be fertile. The season of these floods, is both the spring and the Autumn.

From the[ir] appearance the houses of this village are almost all of new foundation, and the land nearby is almost entirely uncultivated. At about fourteen miles' distance from Trips=hill we once again crossed the river to the South [side], in order to take the best way; which is itself almost constantly traveled on the plains near the river's banks. These plains are all cultivated, and entirely free of trees, and the soil is of an extraordinary goodness. We observed that the main harvest is of *grano d'India* [corn], and of oats: there is also a small portion of wheat. In general these plains occupy the entire bottom of the valleys, and are consequently [*37*] now wide and or narrow.

38. Groat's (originally DeGroot's).
39. Tribes Hill.

Six miles to the west from the place where we crossed the river, one arrives at the village called Fort plain, which is composed of but a few homes and a Church, and inhabited by Germans, similarly of such extraction are almost all the households encountered from here on-ward for about forty miles. The Fort which gave the name to the site is entirely destroyed, and there is also difficulty to-day to discover its [floor-]plan. It was built with earth, and its situation was advantageous to command the navigation of the river.[40]

6.d°.   Exiting from the village described, one begins at once to ascend a hill, and almost always for twenty and more miles the road goes now descending and or climbing little hills of rocks which are found within reach of the observation of the traveler. They are of stone of *lorna* grey=blackish, and some of limestone with a fine and tight grain, and of a greyish color.

In this day we advanced about twenty-[*38*]eight miles, always pass-ing through a country almost everywhere cultivated and well popu-lated. At about half of this course, the road departs somewhat from

Figure 9. The road along the Mohawk River at Anthony's Nose. From *The New-York Magazine; or, Literary Depository*, March 1793. (Courtesy General Research Division, New York Public Library, Astor, Lenox and Tilden Foundations)

40. The fort in question was actually Fort Rensselaer. Locals disliked General van Rensselaer and successfully suppressed the fort's official name. Roberts, *New York's Forts*, 383–84.

the river and passes over a little hill, upon whose leveled ground there are built various homes of farmers. This hill takes the name of Fall=hill, because the river in its vicinity makes a little fall with some rocks.[41]

In these neighborhoods every farmer cultivates a number of *Erables** called in English *Maple tree* in order to thus procure the quantity of sugar necessary to his own family. The cultivation of this tree does not require any toil, and the method of extracting the juice is one of the simplest. In the springtime[#] an incision is made to the bark of the tree, about one foot above ground, in conical shape, in such a way as to facilitate the method of extracting the juice which is thus released.[†] This sap is collected in vases, and it is of a whitish color, and a little sticky. The first operation to extract the sweet [*39*] substance which it contains, is to place it in a cauldron and to let the water evaporate.[°] The salty material is deposited on the bottom, and its color is equal to that of the sugar of first purification that is extracted from the canes, that is, of a dark color. Its flavor however differs a lot, and the sugar extracted from this juice has something displeasing, which is however lost if it is purified again. In general the product of this juice is of about 4 to 6 pounds of sugar per 100 lbs. of weight.[§] But this proportion is subject to considerable variation, perhaps depending on the age of the tree, or on the nature of the soil which nurtures it. In Albany we saw a small quantity of this sugar perfectly refined, as much as that which is sold on the market under the name of third quality, and then the difference between it and that of the sugar cane is barely distinguishable by the most refined palates. But this refinement costs much, and it would end up being more expensive than this second one. Nonetheless the research begins to be considerable, since the Quakers [*40*] resist using the other one, because it is produced by black slaves.

From the bad tavern kept by Cap. Mayer[42] there are but twelve miles to come to the place denominated Fort Schuyler,[43] but because the more passable road is found on the North side, thus we had again to

---

41. Little Falls.

    * *in French the Acer Saccharinium of Linneus* [PA's note].

    # *from the end of Febr. until the middle of April._ The juice flows in greater quantity when after a night of strong frost, follows a warm day* [PA's note].

    † *These incisions yield liquor for about six weeks containing some saline parts: but it also continues then in the summer to provide a clear liquor, which does not contain saline parts of sugar in sufficient quantity to extract it usefully. Some people utilize this juice as a drink* [PA's note].

    ° *This operation made in the [illegible] hours is much more profitable* [PA's note].

    § *The plants [trees] of florid vegetation yield in the nice days between four and six gallons of this juice* [PA's note].

42. John Mayer.

43. Here, PA uses the original name for this fort where Utica now stands. However, as noted above, Fort Stanwix was also commonly known as Fort Schuyler.

cross the river; But there being on this side neither a bridge nor a boat, we were forced to ford it not without great risk, having swelled from the continuous rains of the preceding days. The road on this side is better but absolutely dangerous not only for a carriage but also for simple horses. It is covered almost its entire length by thick woods which do not permit an easy transit not even in the drought of summer.

A few years ago one could find very few dwellings on this side; but the richness of the soil [41] and the comfort of the vicinity of the navigable river has induced a considerable number of families from New England, and from the other northern provinces to emigrate here, and this number grows very much every year. The roads were covered with men, women, livestock and farm tools of the new colonists. The land on this side belongs mostly to the State of N. York; nonetheless there are some individuals who possess great tracts. The common price is a British pound and 20 shillings per *acre*, that is, twelve *liras* and five *tornesi soldi*[44] per *perto*[45] when the soil is not free of trees, because otherwise the value of the land would be greater. In general every family of these new colonists buys two or three hundred *acres*; and nothing is more laborious than the toil that they have to endure for the first two years, in addition to the illnesses that are usually caused by the first exhalations of the odors of a virgin soil. [42]

They have first to carry with them tools and livestock, not only as many as are needed to help him in their toil, but also to provide for their sustenance the first new months of his settlement. As soon as the colonist arrives at his new property he has to start cutting the plants and small trees that cover the ground upon which he intends to build the first hut for his own personal use and for a small barn for the livestock. Of these materials he makes his dwelling, which is built easily utilizing the trees one on top of the other and closing the gaps with mud mixed together. The bark of the big trees pressed and dried are used to make the roof of the house, and are an excellent cover. This first task occupies the entire family for some months; afterward it is occupied with clearing part of the nearby woods of the smaller trees, leaving the big trees to be cut later, which require a lot of time (Figure 10).

As one part is cut, they pile up the wood and they consume it with fire. Having cleared the woods a little in such a manner [43] they make a circular incision to every great tree and they set it on fire, so as to burn all the leaves, and stop its vegetation. This operation is done to leave free access to the rays of the sun, because in the middle of these

44. Currency from Turin, Italy.
45. More properly *pertica* in Italian, a long wooden stick and an old agrarian measure, used here as an equivalent to the British acre.

trees, they sow at once some *grano d'India* and *pomi di terra* [potatoes], which have to sustain the family the coming year. In winter (winter lasts five or more months) the main occupation is transporting goods on sleds until Schenectady and some up to Albany; and in the spring of the second year they begin cutting the trees, that can be compared to very big giants. Once fallen and cut in two or three pieces, they place them on fire and thus they consume them.

These trees are of different species, but for the most part they are of hardwood and excellent for construction. The length of their trunks and their nice shape is truly surprising. We have measured various of them which surpassed 120 feet in length, to which they set fire.

[*44*] Arrived at the place called Fort Schuyler,[46] whose fortifications are also entirely destroyed. We crossed anew the Mohocks to the South, to gain the road to Oneida, the first of the Indian nations that is found on this side. At six miles farther ahead one finds a new village *28.d°.* called White-bourgh[47] composed of new colonists, and from here there are not more than twenty-one miles to arrive at the first dwelling of

Figure 10. A typical white settler family cabin. From Orasmus Turner, *Pioneer History of the Holland Purchase of Western New York* (Buffalo, N.Y.: Geo. H. Derby, 1850).

46. Fort Stanwix. See note 24 above. This fort had been the site of several important treaties between various Native nations and Great Britain, the United States, and New York State. It had been besieged by the British in 1777 and abandoned in 1781 after being ravaged by fire.
47. Whitestown or Whitesboro.

the savages. All along this road you do not find but two or three families, and since it is across dense forests as if it is always night and since at every moment you encounter trails, trod by Indian hunters, that resemble roads, it is easy for he who does not have a guide or compass to lose his way. Since it is difficult to procure the first, we used the second means, which served us passably well.

[45]   Of Oneida.

━━━

This nation is one of the six confederate ones, that is of the Tuscarora, Senekas, Mohowks, Oneidas, Onondagas, and Delaware,[48] which inhabit a large area circumscribed by the State of N. York, by that of Pensilvania, and by the lakes of Canada', whose ownership is today accorded to them by Instruments [treaties] with the States and by guarantees with the Sovereigns. The limits of their territory are to the South with the East branch of the River Susquehannah, and to the North with the lakes Ontario and Oneida: small rivers to the East and to the West circumscribe the other two limits. Thus they occupy about one degree of latitude and two of longitude.[49] This terrain could easily suffice for the subsistence of a population one hundred thousand times larger than the actual one of these nations, if the inhabitants would dedicate themselves to agriculture, and to live off the products of the soil; but since the savages adjust badly [46] to labor, and they prefer the wandering life and the uncertain sustenance of the chase, thus they complain of the restricted space of territory that they can roam, and quite often while hunting they exit from the prescribed boundaries.

The soil inhabited by these Indians is of the richest and most fertile quality to be found on our globe, and it is generally flat, cut across only from time to time by small rivers and little hills, and full of lakes which abound in fish, and salubrious waters. But except for a few cultivated fields which are found near their dwellings, all the rest is covered by very thick forests, which abound with various species of quadrupeds and birds. The town of Oneida occupies an area of about five miles cleared of trees, in which are found scattered from place to

48. PA misidentified the Delawares as members of the Six Nations and omits the Cayugas.
49. This vague description of territory does not reflect accurately either Oneida or Iroquois territory in 1790.

place some houses of the savages, and its entire population does not amount to five hundred inhabitants.[50]

This nation is one of the oldest [47] in the confederation, with the exception of the Mohowks, and its language differs little from this one, and it has embraced Christianity since the beginning of this century, with the exception of about 1/9 which continues in paganism, and perhaps it might be better to say without any religion of any kind. Whether their embracing of Christianity should be attributed to the greater intercourse that they always had with the European colonists, or to a greater facility to persuasion it would not be easy for us to assert. But we were present at the divine service celebrated by a protestant missionary[51] who resides among them and we were in general surprised by their demeanor and by the agreeable melody of the singing of the psalms, rendered in their language. Those who are Christians observe Sunday[s] with scrupulous attention, abstaining even from games and from the hunt; but the rest laugh at these religious practices, without however it being possible to state that they are worse than the others in their customs. [48] The physical constitution of these Indians is not apt to give of them an idea of great robustness, as among some that inhabit the banks of the Mississippi.[52] The men are thin, and generally of a medium stature; but the women are absolutely weak, small, and very thin. Consequently, since there are few families among the Oneida that have preserved the Indian blood from mixing with that of the Europeans, thus the color of some of them is not as yellow as is found elsewhere, and some have a little more hair on the chin and in the genital parts; because it is not the general custom among them to eradicate it.

Their dress consists of a shirt which reaches toward the middle of the thighs and remains hanging and in the winter they cover themselves with a woolen covering which has the double function of serving as a bed. The thighs are entirely naked; except for a band that passes through them, and thus it covers the reproductive parts. Some

50. Kanon'alohale, or "Head on a Pole," known among whites as Oneida or Oneida Castle. It had been burned by the British and their Native allies in 1780. The Oneidas occupied five villages, of which this was the largest. Samuel Kirkland Papers 140a, Burke Library, Hamilton College, Clinton, N.Y.

51. Samuel Kirkland (1741–1808), a Presbyterian. Kirkland had been laboring among the Oneidas for nearly a quarter-century by the time of PA's visit, although with nothing like the success Andreani attributed to him. Kirkland recorded PA's visit in his diary entries of August 28–30. He wrote, "This young Nobleman is travelling with the laudable view of improving his mind, & storing it with useful knowledge." Walter Pilkington, ed., *The Journals of Samuel Kirkland*, 202–3.

52. In comparing the Oneidas to Indians of the Mississippi, PA drew upon his encounters with Creeks and Cherokees at Halifax and New York City.

of them wear a sort of woolen boots and leather shoes; [49] but this is not usual except among the most wealthy, and especially in winter. In the days of parade [on festive occasions] they adorn themselves with silver ornaments like collars, bracelets, bells, etc., and the women, who do not differ from the men except in having a corselet which rounds around their thighs, love to adorn themselves with feathers, ribbons and bizarre ornaments of every kind, creating all together an elegant dress.

Among the men are often found some who make a crown on their head with animal feathers, or with flowers, and others load their heads with a prodigious quantity of fake hair which falls decorated and curled in every direction, and which disfigures them entirely. In this nation today few are those who are in the habit of painting themselves, and those few are found among the men, our having observed only two women who had a red line painted across their heads, and a bit of color on their cheeks. Among the men this painting requires a great deal of time, since they [50] execute it with elegance, now featuring ribbons of different colors, now pictures of animals. This bizarre usage, common to all the nations of savages, must have had its origin in the parts of the South where the soil is covered by an immense quantity of mosquitoes of all qualities and species [which] has forced the inhabitants to find a means by which to preserve themselves from the bites of those bothersome animals. Once this usage started to spread, it must have very soon become common among the nations of the North where these animals are smaller in number, and less stinging, since it was introduced as part of the ornamentation of the warriors, in order to thus inspire fear in the enemy with a flaming face. We have made various researches on such a usage, in different circumstances, and we received the same answer, which lends itself very well to the probability [of being correct].

The other bizarre custom among the Indians is of cutting the ears in different strips and of ornamenting themselves [51], the nostrils, the lips etc. with pieces of silver or with all sorts of ornamentations, but this latter usage begins to be disregarded among the Oneidas. The cutting of the ears is peculiar only to the men, and it is among these to those who are called warriors; but since in this class are numbered almost all of the inhabitants, thus it was improperly believed that this custom was absolutely part of the ornamentation of the savage male.

It is believed that the origin of this custom was to demonstrate that they have no revulsion to shedding their own blood, nor to suffering, and certainly this operation is very painful, especially as it is performed with only common scissors. During the time of our sojourn in this nation we were present at one of these operations; and the young man of about fifteen years who was suffering it yelled like an eagle, so loudly and acutely, that his cries were heard at several miles' distance. We have seen an Oneida, the lobes of whose ears fell nine inches and seven lines [eighths of an inch], and the ornaments that he carried hanging [52] on each side, weighed seven ounces.

We have reported earlier that the physical constitution of the [female] sex in this nation is poor, and having endeavored to investigate the reason, we could not assign one other than the custom of breastfeeding the offspring for about two and more years, which must contribute naturally to weakening the mother and the child, and perhaps also to their tiring labor; since they cultivate the fields, they cut the wood, they build part of the house, and in travels in winter they carry on their shoulders the children and the household tools. That such a long nursing of the offspring must contribute to weakening them appears to us to be beyond question, and we observed a child of twenty-seven months, who was nourished entirely of the mother's milk, and under the appearances of robustness, and of good health; he absolutely could not stand on two feet.

Figure 11. Oneida family (with two views of female), 1809, by the Baroness Hyde de Neuville. (Courtesy New-York Historical Society)

It is but at the age of three that they begin to walk on their own. [*53*] The more common diseases in this nation are inflammatory fevers caused by the immoderate use of strong liquors and various kinds of venereal diseases. Decoctions of different herbs help the first and the second of these disorders, and decoctions of medicinal plants are the remedy for all other illnesses, complicated or simple. Which are the herbs they make use of in these different circumstances we cannot assert, since the doctor was absent from the village for several months, and because this class keeps a kind of professional secret, thus the nature of the medicinal plants is not explained but to those who pay to be initiated.[53]

It is always a difficult feat to divine the nature of the illness; and since even the more able practitioners of the [medical] art among ourselves often are deceived, thus it should not be surprising if some ignorant savages do not succeed. The missionary who resides for more than twenty-five years in this nation has assured us that in the complicated illnesses, few are healed. What has surprised me was [*54*] to be assured that the venereal disease, even the more complicated, is cured in four or five days. An old man of about sixty told us he was himself infected, and before our departure he was perfectly healed in terms of the external sores. It would remain to examine whether the healing was as complete internally. We shall have occasion in time to observe this fact more accurately.

The frequent intercourse that this nation had with the European colonists, and the religious principles with which they have become accustomed since after they embraced Christianity, have influenced greatly their customs; and we can call the Oneidas savages half civilized, and although some of them do not profess any religion, nonetheless living together, produced an overall equality.

Hospitality is common to all Indians, and it is [*55*] truly to be admired the earnest attention they express on the occasion of the visit of a stranger. Then the entire family is engaged for him, and the men go out to hunt to procure sufficient provisions. Among themselves in the family they love each other greatly, and their filial love is no less than that which exists amongst ourselves.

In marriages there is no formality of any sort. Whenever the parties are happy they unite without celebrating any sort of rite, as long as the missionary does not oblige them to renew the act in the Church, which often occurs to be after the consummation; and those who are Christians do not separate from their wives except in case of proven

53. PA's discussion is predicated upon a rather ethnocentric conception of medicine and medical practitioners. James W. Herrick, *Iroquois Medical Botany*, ed. Dean R. Snow (Syracuse, N.Y.: Syracuse University Press, 1995), 82–85.

adultery; this however happens less than one would think, in a country where the women have all the most possible freedom, and where
they are left for several months alone, while the husband is obliged to
[undertake] far away runs [travels]. But it is not true that in a similar
case the separation is generally observed. Often the husband is satis-
fied with beating the wife.

It is true that in the days of [56] public feasts, or dances, which usually occur on the occasion of some treaty or of [the visit of] some
foreigner, these disorders, as well as others of a different kind, are frequent, because the Indian, who does not have the means to procure
for himself a daily use of liquor, uses it with excess when it becomes
easily available, and then the women who also participate with pleasure are more cheerful, and more libertine, while some men end up
quarreling among themselves and beating each other up. The end of
a dance is always crowned with blood, and it frightens whomever wit-
nesses it for the first time.[54]

The Oneidas are like all Indians, lovers of laziness; and we think
that they would not go out to hunt if necessity did not force them to.
These [Indians] have taken some liking to agriculture, and almost every
family cultivates a vegetable field and one of *grano d'India*, but in this
labor the men are rarely involved. [57] They stay home lying down
and smoking, or enjoying themselves with friends in some game, while
the wife ruins in the hardest labor in the field. At night they go to
sleep early, sleeping on bare benches, covered only with a blanket;
and they get up early in the morning. The first activity consists of sit-
ting by the fire smoking, if in the winter, or near smoking [embers] if
in the summer; and here they converse amongst themselves of public
affairs, of which they are eternally occupied, even though they do not
have much to keep them busy. This smoking that they have the habit
of doing around the houses is to protect themselves from the insects.

After some time thus spent, often they go out with the gun, or with
the bow to the hunt; and in the meantime the wife puts to boil a ket-
tle of *grano d'India* with some vegetable, in the amount necessary
for the use of the family for the entire day. If the hunter was lucky,
he returns with the prey, and often he leaves it in the field where he
killed it [58] and he sends the wife to retreive it; because it would be
humiliating for him to carry a burden, when he has [one] who must

---

54. Drinking often accompanied the payment of the annuities derived from federal
and state treaties on or around June 1. In 1793 the Oneidas' schoolteacher, Ebenezer
Caulkins, observed, "Since the Indians received their money this place has been almost
a little H-ll on earth." Caulkins to Israel Chapin, June 20, 1793, vol. 9, O'Rielly Papers,
New-York Historical Society.

do it. Thus a man carrying wood would be scorned by all the neighbors. After all this he lies down on the bed, and without asking anything he expects to be served the meal when it is ready; and then the wife calls all the children to share what there is, and having made equal portions everyone takes his and eats when it most pleases him. In general the hour of the meal is around four or five P.M.

Oneidas are only hunters; they are little or not interested in fishing, even though there is a beautiful lake in their territory that bears the same name full of excellent fish, and which extends for twenty-five miles from East to West; and the best time for the hunt are the six months of the winter. Bears, deer, fallow deer, and martens are the only animals of which they go in search, because their skins [59] are sold in the markets; and during the hunting season they nourish themselves for the most part with the meat of these animals. Some white people who spent some time with the Indian hunters told us that the meat of the bear# after it has been well boiled is of an excellent taste. They make use alternatively of the gun and the bow, and they use both these instruments of death with remakable skill. For the most part in the hunt they are accompanied by their friends, and in case these are either unlucky or unskilled, they divide their kill out of good will as long as no one refuses to work at the cleaning and first preparation of the skins.

In the months of harvest this nation does not go out [to hunt], except in case of some extraordinary need; and during this time the men amuse themselves almost every day at a game which consists of making a ball jump.[55] Every player is equipped with a kind of racquet about four [60] feet and six inches long, which in the lower end curves considerably, and thus stretching a string of the bow it serves to throw the ball. One who catches it with this instrument and thus making it jump; he prevents others from touching it until he is able to make a certain number of rounds of a large field; he is the winner. This game requires agility at running and dexterity; and we have attended one such game which lasted two-and-a-half hours, during which a great sum was wagered by both sides.

The other amusements consist of at times running on foot and at times on horseback to a certain destination. When those games are performed for money or goods, then the women are present, and they proceed with horrible yells to incite the party in which they have interest.

In our voyage along the great lakes in the North-West of Canada', we were forced to make use of this nourishment that we experimented [found to be] of bad taste, and unhealthy. The small bears *are a little more* tolerable [PA's note].

55. Lacrosse.

The idleness of these Indians is so great that we have seen one of them run for about seven hours on horseback around a field, dressed up in a way to be [*61*] recognized by his friends only with difficulty, thus serving as a clown [amusing] those who saw him. We couldn't help noticing that he was a Warrior, and therefore respected in the nation.

It would be difficult to speak clearly of the government of this nation, since those who have visited it often themselves, or who resided here for a length of time, have never bothered to examine its principles. We had much difficulty to acquire some general notion during our stay. There are two kinds of offices, the one hereditary within the families, the other is conferred solely on the basis of pure merit; and those who are entrusted enjoy great authority within the nation, and in the councils. Three are the chiefs of the first class, and the number of the second is undetermined.

The succession to these hereditary offices is not established but in the sons of the females to the exclusion of the males so that the son of a sister is preferable to one's own son. This heir to the title of chief must be nominated [*62*] by the predecessor while he is still alive; but sometimes as he dies without having nominated him, the council convenes, and it chooses him from among the closest relatives of the deceased, always observing the law of female descent. The chiefs elected by merit, are thus by the council, and all have to be in agreement. A good warrior, a good politician, a good orator, is elected Chief Warrior and sits in the council. Sometimes a simple action that would be everywhere deemed as madness may among the Oneida Indians lead one to be esteemed a chief, f.[or] e.[xample], one who crossing an immense territory arrives in a faraway nation, [and returns] carrying some sign of his arrival there, could be, and often is, esteemed a chief.

When among the hereditary chiefs the elected one should still be a boy, then he must be present at the council for five years without liberty to speak, and a tutor speaks and acts for him. [*63*] This nation does not have written laws, either civil or criminal: nonetheless there are often examples of thefts, of wrongdoing, and of homicides. Relative to this, we are often amazed by the small number of inhabitants that comprise this nation. In the first case the thief has nothing else to suffer but public disgrace, because when it is triggered it is so great that he is obliged to expatriate.

In the case of a homicide, the killer has nothing to fear from the government, and has only to guard himself from the machinations of the closest relative of the deceased to whom exclusively is given [the right] to avenge the offense; and if he is a man of courage he never fails, ambushing the offender in some narrow passage, and killing him

there. In every similar case the council gathers and procures with advice to prevent similar consequences. With regard to the civil laws they
are also unwritten, but they are observed with a wise [*64*] reasonable-
ness. In case one dies without successors the council gathers and divides
the property of the deceased among his friends in equal parts; and if
he has direct descent then he passes the substance to the natural heirs.

In building this nation has embraced the practice of the neighboring europeans, and instead of building a rectangle [longhouse] with
various niches inside in the same way they practiced before, they now
build one single small house in which they place various berths. As far
as we are concerned we regard their original method as the best, except for the fireplace, which being situated in the middle of the room
is more subjected to smoking. (S[ee]. the design Vol. II.)[56]

The population of Oneida amounts to no more than seven hundred
souls, among whom about one hundred and fifty are soldiers (fighting
men) the major part of whom live in the town by the same name. A few
years ago [*65*] this nation was diminishing rapidly every year, but
according to a register kept by the missionary it has been growing
for the last six years. Having made some inquiries into their color and
the tradition [of the impression] made upon them by the sight of
the first white man, I was assured that these latter ones were then denominated *eskéànt*, that is men without blood.[57] They call themselves
however *Ongwéhoerwe*, that is true men.[58] When some foreigner of distinction comes to visit their country, the chiefs gather promptly in
council to decide whether he should be complimented or not. Sunday
after the evening service they all gathered, and after some time we
were invited to stop by the place of assembly. We entered a miserable
hut where we found that the chiefs, about twenty-five in number, were
gathered and seated according to their rank. Among the first we distinguished *Skannondóa*[59] who had lodged us [*66*] in his house and received us with the greatest hospitality. He invited us to sit by his side,
and made us tell whether we had anything to say to the nation. The

56. PA drew a sketch in volume 2, now unfortunately lost.
57. This word (jéskvn) translates more closely to a skeleton standing, living skeleton, or ghost (RW).
58. This word (ukwehu:wé) translates more closely to original human (RW).
59. John Skenandoah (1706–1816) was a Pine Tree chief of the Oneida wolf clan.
His name as produced here (oskvnu:tú:) is a diminutive of the word for deer (RW). He
was a close confidant of Kirkland's and assisted the United States during the Revolution until his imprisonment at Niagara. He played a prominent role in Oneida relations
with whites in the war's aftermath. Laurence M. Hauptman, *Conspiracy of Interests: Iroquois Dispossession and the Rise of the Empire State* (Syracuse, N.Y.: Syracuse University
Press, 1999), 42–44; Julian Ursyn Niemcewicz, "Journey to Niagara, 1805," ed. and
trans. Metchie J. E. Budka, *New York History* 44 (1960): 95.

interpreter passed the compliment that we made, after which the first among the chiefs harangued us in these terms "Father (thus they are used to addressing foreigners[60]) we Your children are always happy and disposed to receive amicably those who come in the *Great=canoes* (thus they call the ships) from the other side of the Great=Lake / the sea / to visit the Oneidi, and we pay you compliment that God had preserved you from many dangers that are encountered in such an immense journey, and that you have come to us safe. Conserve, O Father, the love that Your Brothers have always shown toward us, and that we may always be at peace. The Kings, the Chiefs, the Chief Warriors thank you for your visit, and they pray you to stay with them in the Great Island until the sun will turn." At the end of this discourse the chief that had pronounced it got up from his place and came to shake my hand, [*67*] which that afterward did all the other ones one by one. Since they then had to discuss business thus we took leave and we left them in council.

====

Of the Tuscaroras.

If we shall say but a few words about this nation, it is because in reality they differ very little from that of which we have spoken, as well for the brief residence we have made among them. This nation is composed of only about eighty families and the number diminishes every day, and they are incorporated in the six nations since not too long ago, they being originally of North Carolina and Virginia. Always persecuted by wars, they were obliged to go wandering for a long time, until they were received by the Oneidas, and incorporated under the supposition that they would be a branch of it [*68*] since some analogy was found in the language.[61] Today they live to the North West of Oneida, and follow almost the same customs.

60. In fact, the term "father" was generally reserved for Frenchmen as opposed to Englishmen and Americans. The Oneidas probably associated Andreani with France since he looked and sounded more like a Frenchman than an Englishman or Anglo-American. However, they may have recalled Italy's minor contributions to French missionization and warfare in Iroquoia.

61. The Tuscaroras began to emigrate after the Tuscarora Wars (1711–13) and were formally adopted into the Iroquois League in 1722 or 1723. After the Revolution most Tuscaroras resettled at Niagara. David Landy, "Tuscarora among the Iroquois," *Handbook of North American Indians*, vol. 15 (Washington, D.C.: Smithsonian Institution Press, 1978), 518–24.

=====

Of the Onondagas

=====

). d°. The road that passes from Oneida to the capital town of this nation
is about thirty miles long, and traverses obscure and dense forests,
among which we encountered every moment bears and rattlesnakes.*
A big dog attacked one of these animals, and was bitten by it. An
Indian who was accompanying us followed it on horseback between
the woods, reached it, and killed it. It was of a monstruous size, and
had twenty-nine knots in the tail. Thus poisoned, the wounded leg of
the dog began to swell, and when the swelling reached the head, he
died amidst the most acute spasms and pains. He lived but forty-two
minutes after he was bitten. From this example [*69*] it can be induced
how great the caution of travelers should be, and the same of inhabitants, since even if it were possible to cure the wound, if the remedy
is not the most expeditious possible, it would do no good. The guides
invited us to follow the tracks of a bear, and to witness their skill. He
was of an ordinary size, and even though he was near to the cubs that
he wanted to defend, nonetheless as soon as he received a little wound
from the first shot, instead of rushing against the aggressor or trying
to defend himself, he ran away, but since he was losing a lot of blood
it was easy to kill him.

The principal village of this nation, which assumes the name of the
nation itself, is neither so considerable nor so populated as that of
Oneida.[62] The homes are almost all constructed the Indian way, as it
better appears from the design, some of which are more than sixty
feet in length, and have four [*70*] fireplaces at different intervals.

In the lower divisions they lay down at night to sleep, and they
spend the day gathered in the same clearing near the fire. The cubi-
cles above are used to keep domestic tools, and the provisions.

The inhabitants of this nation are not hunters, but rather pursue
fishing, and when we visited them, few familes had returned; the
remaining were expected momentarily. They spend four months out

---

* *In Italian they are otherwise called Caudisono* [PA's note].

62. Onondaga (also known as Onondaga Castle) had been destroyed by the Conti-
nental Army in the spring of 1779. The repopulated village was home to approximately
one hundred Onondagas. Harold Blau, Jack Campisi, and Elisabeth Tooker, "Onondaga," *Handbook of North American Indians*, 15:491–99.

of the year in this occupation, and they prepare the principal nour-
ishment for the winter. A part of them fish in Lake Onondaga, and
others travel farther, some to the Seneka River, others in the little
rivers that are found between their lake and that of Ontario. The Lake
of Onondaga is about six miles long, and has an unknown depth. The
hills that surround it are little elevated and pleasant, and if they were
cultivated and populated they would present a picture of the most
picturesque.

Near this lake on its east side are [71] various springs of water
strongly impregnated with common salt, which it seems to us denotes
some great mass of fossil salt enclosed deep into the earth, since the
sea is too far removed to suggest a communication between it and
said springs. A white man has obtained from the Indians permission
to make salt at one of these springs, and has established forty-eight
boilers with which he extracts two thousand pounds of salt a day, and
since the wood necessary to evaporate the water costs but the work of
cutting it thus the profit is great.[63] One hundred pounds of water contain about 34-36 of salt.

This nation cultivates even less soil than the Oneidas and therefore

Figure 12. An eighteenth-century Iroquoian longhouse. Detail from Plan du
Fort Frontenac ou Cataraouy, ca. 1720. (Courtesy Newberry Library)

63. Citizens of New York claimed the right to share the saltworks with the Onondagas on the basis of a treaty signed in 1788. In 1790 there were three men harvesting salt
there, Asa Danforth, Comfort Tyler, and Nathaniel Loomis. Salt sold at one dollar per
bushel. Hough, *Proceedings*, 199; Joshua V. H. Clark, *Onondaga; or, Reminiscences of Earlier and Later Times*, 2 vols. (Syracuse, N.Y.: Stoddard and Babcock, 1849), 2:10.

it is even poorer, being obliged to buy various articles of first sustenance. For the rest it differs little in customs from these latter ones,
except in the religion, they not having embraced Christianity like
[*72*] these [the Oneida]. In case of homicide or theft they behave in
the same manner we have described in speaking of Oneida, and similarly in the succession of offices and in matters of inheritance.

They have a notion of a Supreme Being, who must have created the
world, and punishes after death those who have behaved badly. The
future life according to them consists of a continuous wandering over
the world, now enjoying it, if deserving of a reward, or suffering if
deserving of punishment.

The religious ceremonies are limited to only one day a year in the
month of January, and consist of sacrificing three white dogs, and one
barrel of tobacco. The people, preceded by their chiefs, gather around
a great fire and after they have decorated the victims with flowers, they
throw them in the flames, the chief pronouncing these words "These
animals that we are sending you may please you oh Avenniyo," [*73*]
(God[64]); and then throwing a few packets of tobacco "And this tobacco
to serve You for smoking." The ceremony ends with dancing around
the sacred fire, singing at the same time some hymn, which for lack of
having a good intepreter we could not have translated.

In marriage there is no religious formality whatsoever; thus also
some live with two wives, and they change them at will. It is rare that
a man finishes [his life] with the first wife. Whenever a man separates
from his wife [she] takes with her but a single male son, and often
refuses to take anyone at all; they all remain on the shoulders of the
husband.[65] In the funerals there is not any great ceremony; but only
the neighbors and at times the entire village gathers in the home of
the deceased, but they bring their own provisions, and they entertain
themselves with a banquet. What should be the origin of this custom
[*74*] we were not able to discover.

We shall finish that which we have said about the Indians of the Six
Nations, by reporting here below a small vocabulary, and some principal rules of their grammar.

64. The Iroquoian word provided (haweNnijo) translates approximately to "his
voice/word is good" (RW).

65. As with so much about Iroquois culture, PA apparently misunderstood; the
phrase should indicate that the children all remained with the woman. Gretchen
Green, "Gender and the Longhouse: Iroquois Woman in a Changing Culture," in
Women and Freedom in Early America, ed. Larry D. Eldridge (New York: New York University Press, 1997), 7–25; Elisabeth Tooker, "Women in Iroquois Society," in *Extending
the Rafters: Interdisciplinary Approaches to Iroquois Studies*, ed. Michael K. Foster, Jack
Campisi, and Marianne Mithun (Albany: State University of New York Press, 1984),
109–21.

═══

The Mohawks language, of which the Oneida is but a derivation, has some general rules. Their inhabitants when they speak never close their lips, from which it follows that they do not make use of labial letters.

a e and *i* they pronounce like the Italians.

The Moho'ks pronounce the letter *r*, but never the letter *l*; and the Oneida pronounce the latter in place of the former. The Senekas make use of neither one [nor] the other, substituting instead the *h*. For example, the

Mohocks,	*Raniha*, [ra7ni.ha] for *Father*,	
Onida,	*Laniha*, [*la7ni.ha] [75]	
Seneka,	*Hanih*, [ha7nih *WC2039*]	

Often an entire sentence is expressed by a single word. For a better understanding of the few words listed in the following vocabulary, and to facilitate the correct pronunciation, they have been accented. The grave (`) is placed on long syllables; and the [acute] accent (´) on short ones. This language abounds in gutturals, some of which are pronounced more strongly, and others more softly. In the former case they are expressed thus *gh*, in the latter, *hh*.

The two following examples show the use of R, L, and H by the three nations.

Mohocks,	Raweagh, [ra:wvh]	He said
Oneida,	Laweagh,	[lawvh]
Seneka,	Haweagh, [ha:wv:h *WC409*]	

Mohoks,	Raòsare,[rao;share7]	his knife
Oneida,	Laosale, [lao;shale7]	
Seneka,	Hogányaasaith, [hogánya7sæ:7 *WC942*]	
		[76]

Personal pronouns[66]
iih, [i;] I, ise, [ise;] you,

---

66. These paradigms are incomplete. The freestanding personal pronouns lack the feminine indefinite *akaouh(h)a and the first- and second-person dual forms *onge-nouha and *senouha. The possessive personal pronouns lack all but the first and second person singular forms (which are no doubt cited to illustrate the patient prefixes of all the freestanding pronouns except the anomalous first- and second-person singular forms) (RW).

laouhha, [laulha;] he, aouhha, [aulha;] she, ongyouhha, [ukyulha;]
we, tsyouha, [cyulha;] you [plural], Lonouhha, [lonulha;] they,
mascul[ine], onouhha, [onulha;] they, feminine.
Agwawea, [akwa(:)wv.] my/mine, sawea, [sa(:)wv.] your/yours,
active verb[67], [To] Say,
Wagilou, [wa7ki;lu7] I say,
Wahsilou, [wahsi;lu7] you say,
wahhelou, [wahv;lu7] he says
wagealou, [wa7kv;lu7] she says, fem.
Waaggnilou, [wa7akni;lu7] we two say,
Wisinilou, [wisini;lu7] you two say,
wahnilou, [wahni;lu7] they two say, masc.,
waggnilou, [wa7kni;lu7] they two say, fem.
Pl. Wagwealou, [wa7akwv;lu7] [we pl. say]
Wissewea[lou], [wisewv;lu7] [you pl. say]
Wahhoni[lou], [wahvni;lu7 (*-hun-)] [they pl. say] masc.,
Wagoni[lou], [wa7kuni;lu7] [they pl. say] Fem.
Pres. Wagélone, [wa7ki;lu7] I said, &c
F. Engilou, [vki;lu7] I will say,
Agilou, [aki;lu7] I can say,
Aougweauge, [aukwvke;] I could, or, I would like to have said
Aiseauge, [aisvke;] you could, or, would like to have said
Ahaweauge, [ahawvke;] they could, or, would like to have said.
[77]
Ayalou, [ayai;lu7] they could say
Waailou, [wa7ai;lu7] they say
Yondou, [yu:tu.(he7 devoiced)] it is said.

Declension[68]

Laniha, [la7ni.ha]	Pater,
Lageníha, [lake7ni.ha]	my father
Yaniha, [ya7ni.ha]	your father
Sagg'neníha, [shukni7ni.ha (*sha-)]	father of us two
T'waníha, [twa7ni.ha]	our father

67. This active verb paradigm shows the three roots of the suppletive verb "Say": 1.
the momentive [punctual] root –ihru- in the factual [aorist] translated present or past,
and in the other modal tenses; 2. the stative [perfective] root –v- with modalizer –k-,
translated as a perfect conditional; 3. the habitual [serial] root –atu- in the indefinite
subject form, translated as a passive (RW).
68. This "declension" of the noun "father" shows inflection for possessor (not for
case, as is usual in European grammars); it is incomplete, omitting the forms for third-
person singular and feminine nonsingular, as well as for first-person exclusive plural
and inclusive dual, and for second-person dual (RW).

Swaniha, [swa7ni.ha]   your [father]
Lodiniha, [loti7ni.ha]   their father.

=====

Some nouns in these languages:[69]
Italian   Onoida,   and Senekas

=====

God	Niyoh, [*< Mohawk < Huron	(n)dio < French Dieu]
	or, Raweniyo,[lawvniyo.]	Háveniyo [*WC1816, 297*]
The Earth	Oghwheatsya [ohwv.cya7]	Owéentja [*WC1440*]
The Sun [*78*]	Kalaghkwa [kala.hkwa7]	Káahkwa [*WC336*]
The moon	Eghnida [ohni;ta7 *vh-]	Owenida [*WC445*]
The star	Ojestock [oci.stok]	Ajestock [*WC868, 1381*]*
The tree	Kálonda [ka:lu.te7 *-u:ta;]	Kéonda [*WC1946*]
The world	Oghwhentsyagwekow[70],	does not exist in Seneka
The father	Laniha [*la7ni.ha]	Hánih [*WC2039*]
Son [someone's]	Ondadyéa, [utatyv.ha]	
his son,	Loyéa, [loyv.ha]	
Daughter	Sagoyéa, [shakoyv.ha]	
Mother	Agnòlha, [aknulha; *-nol-]	Noiyéah [*WC1213*]
Man [human]	Ongwe,	Ongwe [*WC1458*]
Woman	Onheghtyea [*unhehtyv]	Agouheghtyea [*WC1443, 703*]
Young woman	Kayádáse [kaya;tase7]	
Young man	Laxáá [laksa;]	
Young woman	Ixáá [yeksa; *iksa;]	

69. This vocabulary seems to have been provided to Andreani by Kirkland. Several doubtful or impossible forms and other errors might indicate imperfect competence on Kirkland's part. This would be reinforced by two Oneida speakers' low opinion of Kirkland's pronunciation. Timothy Pickering to Jeremy Belknap, June 16, 1796, 6:187, Timothy Pickering Papers, Massachusetts Historical Society, Boston.

70. [ohucyakwe:ku. *ohwvc- *uhwvc-] "the whole world," was copied in PA's clean manuscript, reading "-toy-" for "-tsy-" [with a round script small <s>] of the original field notes. This indicates that the copyist, probably PA, did not really know the language, or had forgotten what he knew by the time he copied his notes (RW).

Grain (Corn) O'nuste[71] [o:nv.ste7]
Gold   Osinkwala, [oci;nkwal(a7)] meaning yellow
Silver   Oghwísta, [ohwi.sta7]
[79]
Iron   Kanhyouhughgwe[72] [*kanyoN7oN.kwi <WC642,601 inst?]
Water   Oghnèga [ohne:ka;]
Fire   Ojiste [oci.ste7]
Rain   Ogeanolághsela [okvnole.hsla7 *a.h? *v.h??]
Dry   Yostatheagh [yosta.thv]
Humid   Yonánaweagh [yona;nawv]
Winter   Góghseláge [kohsla;ke with Moh. epenth. –e-]
Summer   Agenhage [akvnha;ke]
Spring   Teyogenhòndi, [teyokvnhu.ti <-tye] or,
early spring Keangwédíghtsi, [kvkwite.hci]
Autumn   Kannenage [kanvna;ke]
Church   Onóghsadogeághte [onuhsatokv.hti]
Milk   Ononda [onu;ta7]
Fish   Kentsiyoh [kv.ci7 <-cyu7]
Bread   Kanataloh [kana;talok]
Wine   Onegweághtala n kagh, [onikwvhtalahne:ka;]
              this signifies a liquor of red color, and it is a
              common expression. The following name is more
              expressive, [80] more elegant, and sacred.
              Pronounced properly it does not have that
              harshness that at first sight it would appear to have.
              Oheahhaladasehhouhtselággelé[73] [o7nvhalatahsat-
              uhcela.kele7 –ahsehtu-? *-ahsehu-]
Cow   Teyonhóghshwalonde [teyonhu.hskwalute7 *-ho.hs-]
Horse   Yagoghsatas [kohsa:tv.s *yako-] means a creature that
              carries something on its back. This animal has received
              in the diverse countries of the savages
              different names, according to the impression that it
              made on their spirit [mind] the first time they saw it.
              Thus the Senekas call it Kayendanéghkwe, [WC1946,
              1146] that is, animal that carries on the back.
              The wild animals they call Kállíyo [ka.lyo7].

71. The Oneida word means (Indian) corn, i.e., maize (RW).
72. Unattested for "European instrumental material" except in Seneca (RW).
73. This contains morphemes best paraphrased as "grape-bruising" (or "grape-hiding"?) and "smelly" (RW).

The following are some sentences in the Onaida language, which are most often used by a foreigner[74]

[81]

How are you?   Esghanànktìson e
[* skvnv .. su.he 'peace .. live'? or *vhsatnakti.su7 'finish camp?']
Where do you come from?   Cazzánonquatinonta-se?
[ka.cha7 nukwa;   (*nukwa:ti.) nu:ta.hse7]
Is this the way to Oneida?   Neca-neca-judati Kanónaloale?
[ne; ka.nike7/kvh_nukwa; ayuhtv:ti;/yohtv.ti kana7alo.hale7/*kanu7 ..]
Do me the favor, i.e., Please[75]   Aschitanle. [aski:tv.le7]
I thank you for your civility.   Gniavàn-ne waschitanle.
[yawv./*nyawv. ne waski:tv.le7]
This dish [food] is very good.[76]   Cawalacón - Caniá-ná.
[ka7wahla.ku7 kvh niwa; nv]
How many children do you have?   To nì savilaja?[to; nisawi:la.yv7]
Are you married?   Saniaconcán? [sanyakukv.]
What is your name?   Ot je sajatz? [ot yesa:ya.c]

[82]

Is this your home?   I- seca - sanònsoté?
[ise7kv. sanuhsote.]
Would you give me something to eat?   Atsqui-ne-aschequanonte?
[a.ckwe ne askekhwa.nute7]
I love your daughter.   Chenon wese ne sejana.
[knu;wehse7 ne sheyv.ha]
She is truly beautiful.   Cajátas. [kaya;tas(e7 devoiced)]
If I were an Indian I would marry her.
   Togát conqueónwe acanághe tajonchiátientáchè
[toka.t kukwehu:we. ak(h)e.nyake7/-ena.kle7 tayukyatyv:ta.ke7]
I wish to learn your language.
   Ikèl-e ajaván acalónche-tsi ni suavánnotan.
[i:ke.lhe7 aya:wv; aka;luke7 ci7 niswawvno;tv]
I hope you would not want to trouble yourself.
   Tacán tan con nicònláalan. [ta.kv7 tvku7nikulha:lv;]
I love this country very much.
   Vaconvesquanie ne canto. [*wa7knuweskwa.nye7 ne kv;tho]

74. Andreani hastily collected the seventeen phrases himself from the dictation of Native informant-interlocutors. Some are difficult to interpret (RW).
75. The Italian says "Do me the pleasure," the Oneida "May you have mercy upon/care about me," as in the next entry "that you had../cared.." (RW).
76. The Oneida says "this(?) meat is tasty" (RW).

[*83*]
Little Vocabulary in the Onondagas language

Onondaga	Otiseànagéde	[hotihsvnakehte]
God	Avenniyo	[hawvniyo]
Earth	Vovenga	[uhwvcya7]
sun	Kàlaqua	[kalahkwa7 with Oneida –l-]
moon	the same as the sun, with the epithet *of night*	
		[ahsuthvhkha7 kalahkwa7]
stars	Ozzistennoqua	[ocistvnohkwa7]
a tree	Kalonta	[kaluta7 with Oneida –l-]
People	Ongwe	[ukwe]
Father	Kenìgho	[hake7nih]
Son	Ontatáwa	[*utatha:wah ?]
Daughter	Hé-en	[*(k)heyv7 ?]
Mother	Ahó-hó	[*(a)hoho l*haha]
Man	Longwé	[lukwe with Oneida –l-]
Woman	Ae-én	[*ehv ,*ehru]
[*84*]		
Young man	Laksáa	[laksa7a with Oneida –l-]
Young woman	Exáa	[eksa7a]
Wheat	Onéca	[onvha7]
Gold	Oxinkwala'	[ocinkwala7 with Oneida –l-]
Silver	as in Oneida.	[ohwista7]
Iron	Odegánzla	[otekvchla7 with Oneida –l-]
Cow	Tionsquálunt	[tyonhuskwalut with Oneida –l-]
Horse	Cóssatens	[kohsatvs]
Water	as in On.	[ohneka7]
Fire	Ozista [ocista7]/only the ending differs from On.	
Rain	Ostáluntiun	[ostalutyu with Oneida –l-]
Dry	O'-én	[ohv]
Humid	Iuszatán	[*yo(s)chatv<-v7i?]
Winter	as in On.	[kohsla7ke with Oneida –l-]
Summer	Kagenhage	[kakvnha7ke]
Spring	Kanguitétzi	[kvkwitechi7(ke)]
Autumn	Kannenáge	[kanvna7ke]
Church	as in On.	[onuhsatokvhti]
Milk	Ononása'	[onuhahsa7 <*onuhrahsa7]
[*85*]		
Poison	Oziunda	[*ocyuta7]
Bread	Odaqua.	[orahkwa7/ol- with Oneida –l-??]

[86] From Albany to the Mineral Springs near Saratoga

7. 7bre. The trip from Saratoga to Albany is but thirty-six miles, and because the road is by its nature passable, thus it can be done comfortably in one day. Exiting from this city one takes the road that runs along the river Udson directly to the North which passes through fertile countryside, and a well-populated country. Seven miles farther ahead one crosses the river to take the road of the East for about four miles and there a new village called Troy is found on the opposite banks, which for being of modern founding in these last five years has grown notably and its inhabitants are industrious, businesslike, and already divert a good portion of the traffic to Albany. Small vessels of thirty tons can ascend the river up to Troy, and with some investment it would be possible to render it navigable for vessels of greater tonnage.

[87] Along the way from this village to Lansingburgh, or New City, one enjoys a nice view of the river Udson, and of the Mohocks, which flows into this latter one divided into four grandiose branches. At the place where these two superb rivers unite are formed various little islands, all verdant and fruit-bearing, which add to the beauty of this sight, which would be by itself imposing.

The Mohocks, two miles before it unites with the Udson, presents a sight of the more majestic than it has ever happened us to see, which is as common in this part of the world as it is rare in our rivers of Europe; that is, falls from a height of about seventy five feet creating a pool of water of about four hundred feet wide.[77] A rock somewhat farther advanced in the river and almost in the middle divides the fall, and altering its uniformity renders the picture more pleasing; while other small rocks that are found [88] on the bottom break the water, which rises in a cloud of vapor. The lateral banks of this magnificent cataract are elevated but some fifty feet above the level of the rock from which the river precipitates, and they add to its murmur by closing the pool this way in the form of an amphitheater (Figure 13).

These hills, as well as all those of the nearby area, are of a black and hard slate that can be separated into very thin leaves. We have said heretofore that a little after passing the borough of New City, one crosses the river Udson again to continue the trip on its western banks until Saratoga. In all this interval there was not a single home counted in 1755; today they follow one another almost without interruption, with only a few tracts of land not* cultivated. The hills that are on the

77. Cohoes Falls.
   * We advise once and for all that this refers only to the margins of the roads, or on the banks of the rivers, and of the lakes [PA's note].

road barely deserve the name, since they are only about one hundred feet in elevation, are almost always of the same nature than the rock we have [*89*] just described, and they present nothing remarkable to attract the attention of a naturalist.

As a reward for for the philosophical [scientific] objects that are lacking on this side, the traveler walks continuously on historic terrain because this was the field on which the American Troops distinguished themselves for the first time during the last bloody war. Regarding this subject it should be remembered that in 1777 the British managed to form a cordon between New York and Canada' all along the Northern river and the lakes George and Champlain. If this plan had been conducted by a General more active than Bourgoigne, [it] would not have failed to be troublesome to the cause of Independence, interrupting in such a way the communication between the States of the North and the East with those of the South, which perhaps would not have espoused the common cause. To this end Bourgoine marched from Canada' across the above mentioned [*90*] lakes and advanced until a few miles' distance from Lansingburgh. At his approach, the poorly-disciplined Americans, who found themselves just then in small numbers and without ammunition, retreated quickly, and the English General could have, using some major effort, taken advantage of the moment, beat them, or at least forced them to abandon their supplies.

Figure 13. The Great Falls at Cohoes. From Joel Munsell, *Annals of Albany* vol. 4 (Albany, N.Y.: Joel Munsell, 1853).

Instead of this Bourgoigne stopped for three days, and Schuyler had time to complete the retreat. The aftermath of this affair was more fortunate than ever for the American army which, growing every day and becoming disciplined, did not retreat any more, but instead forced the retreat of the enemy forces. Gates,[78] who succeeded Schuyler in command, took a strong position at Stillwater, up on a hill, thereby dominating the river passage, as well as the covered advances by land. Borgoyne did not relish having to attack the american general in his entrenchments, and even should he have attempted it there is room to suppose that he would have done nothing but lead his people to the slaughter. These [Americans] were twice as numerous, and the fortifications would have compensated for lack of order and discipline. Some accused the english commander of little courage, but [*91*] having examined the terrain and the position of the two armies, we can say frankly that they accused him improperly.

After a few days thus spent in encampments the two armies put themselves on the move, Borgoyne to fortify himself at Saratoga, Gates to force him into action, or to surround him. The English corps that had to protect the retreat, and that formed the rear guard, were defeated in two days, the nineteenth of September,[79] and the seventh of October,[80] and these actions were quite bloody considering the small number engaged in the contest; they cost England supplies, ammunition, and noticeably weakened her forces.[81] Fraser[82] who commanded them lost his life, and his death was wept by his [men]. He was a good soldier and certainly more active and enterprising than the commander.

Examining the position that Borgoyne took [*92*] in setting up camp at Saratoga, it is fair to say that the American army would not have even dared to attack him; or if it had done so it would have fared worse. The English were in control of the more noticeable elevations in the area; and their entrenchments were strengthened by a considerable line of artillery, and by men accustomed to make good use of it. The skill of the American trappers who, when they are in the forests attack without fear of being attacked, would not have served in the assault on a bastion, and would not have withstood the discharge of a battery. Here the English general had nothing better [to do] than await the reinforcements that he had been promised by the great army

78. Brigadier General Horatio Gates (1728–1806).

79. The Battle of Freeman's Farm.

80. The Battle of Bemis Heights.

81. The British force suffered 1,000 casualties, about one-seventh of its total strength. The Americans, 9,000 strong at the outset of the battles and 17,000 strong at the conclusion, suffered fewer than 500 casualties.

82. Brigadier General Simon Fraser (1729–77).

of New York, which furthermore had to bring along sufficient ammunition to resupply the contingent of Borgoyne, who happened to be
lacking everything. If this help had arrived, and if they could have
combined, it would be difficult to say who would have won the action,
but even if it had arrived, the conjunction could [93] not have been
realized without a clash of arms extremely dubious in its outcome. In
the meantime Gates took all the measures to avoid the retreat toward
the North; which would have been fatal in his view; rather, it can be
said with certainty that then the English would have saved themselves
in the forts that are found on lake George and on the banks of the
Champlain which they possessed at the time. To this effect the measures by Gates were wise, and the success corresponded well with
expectations. He made camp atop some hills,[83] from which if it was
not possible for him to dominate the English camp with his artillery,
he could spy upon its movements, and he was outside the range of its
cannon. Colonel Morgan with his favorite corps of Hunters[84] composed of select people had taken up position at the North West, and
these made a daily massacre of the enemies; while General Fellows[85]
with a corps of three thousand men had crossed the river on the
opposite side to block the passage in case it had been attempted.

[94] Thus surrounded, Borgoigne remained inactive for a while
until, being in want of every necessity, he had to capitulate. Six thousand men fit for service, and a good train of artillery and supplies, fell
into the hands of the Americans, who then began to believe themselves soldiers. From that moment on, the affairs of independence
took a good turn and after such a fact word began to spread across
the Atlantic of the colonies in revolt.

From the place where Borgoyne capitulated to the mineral springs,
there are twelve miles of travel, always across forests, and a country
almost completely uninhabited. The few houses that one encounters
are miserable, and the soil is also by its nature sterile. The trees of the
forests are of a poor proportion, nor can they be compared in any way
to those that we visited in the western parts of this State.

At about half way of this [95] travel, about two miles off the road
one arrives at the banks of the lake of Saratoga, which could have at
most ten miles' circumference. From this lake to the mineral springs
there is nothing of interest.

These springs are sparsed [scattered] in a kind of valley surrounded

83. Bemis Heights.
84. Colonel Daniel Morgan (1733–1802) commanded five hundred sharpshooters
known as "Morgan's Rangers."
85. Brigadier General John Fellows (1733–1808).

by very small hills, and are several in number. From time to time some close while others open up, thus their number is not constant. The soil all around is of little fertility, and not apt for cultivation; and the hills are for the most part of a limestone rock of a dark grayish color, with a fine grain which however gives bad lime. In between these limestone rocks, one finds big blocks of *silex*[86] of an excellent quality to make good gunflint.

Across this valley runs a small rivulet that receives the waters from the mineral springs; and because some fish are found in it, it can be judged how few alterations produce the union of these waters containing carbon dioxide. These waters have a pungent taste when they are quickly extracted from the springs, which they owe [*96*] to a good dose of this gas that they contain; which manifests itself sensibly coming up in bubbles to burst on their surface.

The burst of this gas is so strong that placing a lit candle near it, it blows out quickly, and the animals that are forced to stay in contact with it for some time end up losing their lives suffering atrocious pains.[87] That the pungent sensation that this water produces upon the palate when one drinks it is caused entirely by the carbonic gas can be easily proven.

To this end if one takes two vases, and thus transfers for some time the water from one to the other, the air escapes and the water remains tasteless, conserving forever its natural purity/transparency. The thermometer immersed in one of these springs maintains +8,6°, while it was measuring the outside air +13,1°,._ Inside the places from where these waters spring they form deposits of a calcareous substance, in which is found some small quantity of iron; [*97*] what we seem to notice is that this metal is found suspended and kept dissolved by some kind of acid. We will endeavor heretofore a more detailed analysis. That which surprises a foreigner, and that must still surprise anyone

86. French, flint.
87. Morse, *American Geography*, 263–64: "The most noted springs in this state are those of Saratoga. They are eight or nine in number. . . . The prodigious quantity of air contained in this water, makes another distinguishing property of it. . . . A young turkey held a few inches above the water in the crater of the lower spring, was thrown into convulsions in less than half a minute . . . but on removal from that place and exposure to the fresh air, revived, and became lively. On immersion again for a minute in the gas, the bird was taken out languid and motionless. A small dog put into the same cavity . . . was in less than one minute, thrown into convulsive motions . . . when taken out, he was too weak to stand, but soon, in the common air, acquired strength enough to rise and stagger away. . . . A candle repeatedly lighted and let down near the surface of the water, was suddenly extinguished, and not a vestige of light or fire remained on the wick." The unattributed author of these experiments was Samuel Latham Mitchill, who went on to a distinguished career in chemistry. Sigerist, "The Early Medical History of Saratoga Springs," 546.

else born with reflection, is to consider how many doctors dare send the sick to drink the water of these springs, while there is not a thorough analysis of them of any sort, not only that would measure the quantity of its components, but also their quality.

Thus many come here to drink them or to take them as bath without knowing what medicine they are applying to themselves, and we ourselves have found various sick people for whom different remedies were necessary. What the result of such carelessness could be is easily understood without any further detail.

[98] Of the Valley of New Lebanon, Of the Mineral Springs, and of the Quakers called Shakers.[88]

=====

1. d°. The valley of New Lebanon lies to the South East of the city of Albany, distant about thirty miles, famous for its mineral springs, and for the Quakers called Shakers who have there their principal settlement. The road that leads from Albany to this place is poorly kept, and one passes by areas sterile and uncultivated. The soil is not the best to induce new colonists to settle there. The greater part of the hills that one crosses are composed of foliated clayey banks of different hardness and varied color. In between these banks there are to be found some of a calcareous nature, and others of a hard rock, composed of small fragments of schrol and of greenish mica, containing little globes of milky quartz and feld-spath. [99] The shape of this valley is irregular; but near the hill on which the mineral spring spouts, she forms a kind of oval sink, in the middle of whose plain runs a small rivulet, which is formed partly by the spring mentioned above, and partly by other small rivulets that descend from the hills.

These hills are of varying nature; some of foliated clay, and others of calcareous rock dark-gneiss, containing thick veins of whitish feld-spath. In this very same chain of hills, a few miles farther in the interior, near the border with the State of Massachusetts there are various veins of marble, of different colors, of mediocre hardness; and consequently of mediocre shine. The Quakers of whom we shall speak soon make a commerce of it and they work it. The population is sparse

88. Shakerism's founder, Ann Lee, had been a member of a group of radicals who had left the Society of Friends, or Quakers. Although Shakers and Quakers shared some common doctrines, the two groups differed in other important respects and were not connected.

[scattered] in the valley, but the most considerable group of homes is located to the North of the valley, near the place where the mineral water springs.[89]

The bottom from where the spring spouts is composed [*100*] of foliated clayish-calcareous rock, and of little pieces of very fine greisen, almost entirely composed of quartz. The flowing waters deposit a calcareous substance, whitish and light-weight, to which the inhabitants attribute the virtue of healing quickly every kind of wound. Through the cracks through which this water flows some bubbles of air pass continually, which, collected in a vase, have extinguished a candle. This gas has not given this water any sharp flavor, and it is transparent, drinkable, and good for all daily uses, as part of the population does not make use of any other.

We have twice had occasion to measure the temperature, and we have in both circumstances found it to be +17.6°, while the thermometer [out] in full found itself in the first experiment at +14.1°, and in the second at +10.1°. It would be necessary to examine the temperature when the external is greater, to see whether in such [*101*] a circumstance it would be different. With regard to the mineral parts that this water contains, we will conduct a complete analysis later on. The same consideration we have allowed ourselves [in] speaking of the waters of Saratoga applies also to those which we are [now] reasoning [discussing]. Many come every year to drink them and to take them as bath, without their principles being known. Let us now go on to talk about the Quakers.

He who travels far afield beholds things which lie beyond the bounds of belief; and when he returns to tell of them, he is not believed, but is dismissed as a liar.

Ariosto. Orl[ando]. Fur[ioso].[90]

Among the most extravagant, and the most absurd, religious sects that men invented in moments of delirium, we can frankly put that of which we now undertake to speak; nor is there another one today to our knowledge that can be compared to this one. This sect, if the accounts are true, originated in England, or more precisely in England was born Anna Leese,[91] whom we can consider [*102*] to be the

---

89. Lebanon Springs.

90. *Orlando Furioso* by Ludovico Ariosto (1474–1533). *Orlando Furioso: An English Prose Translation*, trans. Guido Waldman (New York: Oxford University Press, 1974), 60. The quote is from the first verse of the seventh canto.

91. Ann Lee (1736–84).

founder; since it does [not] appear that it has been known anywhere in Europe or America before her time. What was the character of this female it is not possible to assert; if we wanted to adhere to her followers we should regard her as the chosen woman, of whom mention is made in the twelfth chapter of revelations of John; while on the contrary her enemies draw a frightening portrait of her, probably exaggerated and both removed from truth. It appears that she and three or four of her followers arrived from Europe in America in one thousand seven hundred seventy four, where after they had wandered for some time in Pensilvannia, and recruited some new followers, they came to the State of New York where they purchased a tract of land in a place called Nisqueunia,[92] about nine miles to the North West of Albany where they remained unnoticed, or if known, they were but imperfectly [*103*] and [only] by the neighbors. In this first establishment they continued their diverse crafts like blacksmithing, and shoemaking, that were the trades of the first founders and the proselytes, and that are also today the principal occupation of the present [members of the sect].

In Nisqueunia they lived quietly until around the [year] one thousand 783, at which time having increased considerably in number and in wealth, some among them removed to the Valley of New Lebanon where their principal establishment is today, and where we visited them. Here they purchased twelve thousand *acres /arpenti*[93]/ of land and have built a nice village, in which reside almost all those who among them found themselves to be artisans. A few who are farmers live scattered in the nearby fields. The novelty of this sect has not failed to attract many followers, and there are counted in this single place up to four hundred: considerable number if one considers that they have only recruited in a sparsely populated country and that since they do not admit the propagation of the species among themselves, thus they are obliged to recruit continuously [*104*] to sustain themselves. Nothing among them there is privately owned, but everything is in common. The leaders keep a common purse, where they place the daily earnings of each individual, providing each one with the necessities: and because one of the religious principles is laboring much, and being industrious, thus it can be easily believed that they never lack money. The eccentricities of these sectarians are not restricted to the matters of their creed, but they extend also to their way of praying. Of this we are going to talk first.

92. Niskayuna.
93. French *arpent*, equivalent to about one and a half English acres, or about 6,000 square meters.

Two are the churches that they have in this village; or to put it better, there are two houses in which they gather on Sundays. In one of
them the novices have free access, and they usually admit to their
gatherings all those whom curiosity brings to assist; while in the other
none enter but the *advanced*, where in time of gathering they do not
admit anyone else. [*105*] Of this second class we shall say but a few
words in what follows; because having to rely on the testimony of one
who perhaps never entered it, we would be subject to error.

12 dº.   The shape of the church in which the first ones gather is properly kept,
but without any ornamentation or image. This would be the proper
place to put the statue of Folly. At eight in the morning they began to
enter, observing the custom of admitting the men from the western
side, and the women through that of the east. As they entered they
took place in good order, standing always on two feet, because there
are but a few benches, and these principally for the use of foreigners,
and forming thus two triangular battalions one composed of men, the
other one of women. One of the leaders was at the center of these two
divisions, and after some convulsive contortions of the head and of
the shoulders, and after [*106*] spitting often, he proffered a few words
in a thunder[ous] and clear voice, but without connection among
them. Here is how he started. "Order Chris-t, ... our health . . .
. . Your example . . . . . ah propriety . . . . . listen to the one who speaks
. . . . . . will you believe him? . . . . ." and similar separated monosylla-
bles. During such an extravagant beginning, they all were attentive
and showed on the outside a religious concentration. Then he added
"prepare yourself for the divine service." Such a preparation consists
of changing the triangular form of the two battalions in[to] two
square ones: but ahead of forming into this second figure the men
took off their jerkins, and rolled up the sleeves of the shirts with two
ribbons, always maintaining the most complete silence. Thus situated,
as we are about to say, facing with the front some leaders of both sexes
who stood lined up along the wall, waiting that the first one among
these would intone a tune in mystic words, or to put it better, in made-
up words, to which both the squadrons started to dance [*107*] forming uniform paces, and turning from time to time and at the same
time all at once on their two feet.[94] In this ball everyone dances by
himself without touching the companion, nor changing configuration,
conserving the same place, beating the feet in cadence, and some
accompanying themselves with singing. The more the dance progresses

94. PA is describing the "Square Order Shuffle," a dance revealed to Elder Joseph
Meacham in a vision. John T. Kirk, *The Shaker World: Art, Life, Belief* (New York: Harry
N. Abrams, 1997), 19–23, 70–81.

the more the fantasies warm up, and then the contortions, and the twistings are taken to excess (Figure 14).

From time to time the leader ends the intonation, and then the dance ends also, all take a rest, without however changing of configuration nor absenting themselves from their respective places, except to remove their clothes. Thus they remain dancing almost the entire day, and we saw them ourselves in continuous contortions, and in continuous motion from eight in the morning until six in the evening.

As strange as the manner in which this sect worships God may seem, if we have to give faith to testimonies that do not seem to be tainted by partiality, it is today neither as ridiculous, nor as scandalous, as it was in times past. [108] Anna Leese introduced many extravagances and many obscenities, of which we feel disgust to only have to make mention of.

At that time in the temple neither order, nor dignity, or propriety was observed. Entered all those members who most pleased her, and while some preached, others lay down on the floor faking convulsive motions, others smoked the pipe, and others spoke among themselves of extraneous things.

During the ball, things not to be believed were committed. Both sexes were naked and they danced together, without decorum or

Figure 14. Shakers dancing. From Henry Howe, *Historical Collections of Ohio*, vol. 2 (Cincinnati, Ohio: C. J. Krehbiel, 1904).

circumspection. But such dishonorable conduct does not occur any longer, and they are every day modifying themselves ever more in their oddities. At the same time as the *novices* are assembled in this church, so the *advanced* are in theirs. Which practices are observed in this, it is not easy to assert. The doors are shut, and no stranger is admitted there; thus the gossip of the neighbors, who want that [*109*] scandals and foolishness are committed, could well be nothing more than bad-mouthing. Here would be the place to report the religious maxims of this sect, and their creed: but we have to confess that after having taken the trouble to read some manuscripts and converse with some of their *leaders*[95] we are quite far from seeing it clearly, and we per-haps have reason to believe that they themselves ignore that which they adore, and that which they believe. One among the more ad-vanced is the general director of the whole congregation; that which he orders, is executed; that which he says, is believed.

Thus he orders to believe in the divine scripture, but at the same time he interprets it as he pleases. They title themselves followers of the second Apparition of Christ, from which it follows that they regard all the other sects as adorers of the antichrist. Thus according to him there have not been men saved since the Apostles left the world. But the more notable point upon which [*110*] they differ the most from any other sect is the observance of the abstinence of the union of the two sexes, admitting among themselves neither marriage, nor propa-gation of the species.

The *growing*, the *propagating* of the scriptures is not to be understood other than the propagation and the growth of the true credence. It is good however that such an observance is observed scrupulously, since we can rejoice that they having to enroll new members to preserve themselves, this absurd and strange sect will be of but brief duration.

If one wanted to deduce the excellence of their religion from their present-day customs, the verdict would be in their favor. But what does it prove other than the power of fanaticism? Their domestic life is excellent. They are frugal in living, laborious and industrious in work. Whether laboring in the fields on rural cultivation, whether they keep busy in the forges of the different manufactures; their fields are better cultivated than those of their neighbors, [*111*] the products of

95. Presumably Elder Joseph Meacham and Eldress Lucy Wright. PA likely reviewed Meacham's *Concise Statement of the Principles of the Only True Church, according to the Gospel, of the Present Appearance of Christ. As Held to and Practiced upon by the True Followers of the Living Saviour, at New-Lebanon, &c. Together with a Letter from James Whittaker, Minister of the Gospel in this Day of Christ's Second Appearance, to his Natural Relations in England* (Ben-nington, Vt.: Haswell and Russell, 1790). Stephen J. Stein, *The Shaker Experience in Amer-ica: A History of the United Society of Believers* (New Haven, Conn.: Yale University Press, 1992), 1–49.

their hands receive a higher price in the markets because they are more perfect than the others. In contracts they are loyal, honest and straight; without losing their natural cleverness and sagacity. In the homes they are friendly among themselves, and the bane of one is the bane of all. If anyone abused the rule of absolute chastity he would be expelled from the congregation; similarly expelled would be a woman who was found to be pregnant. But there are counted only two cases of such doings; which almost surpasses credulity; considering the intimate union with which the two sexes live together without there being separation of habitation. How can one ever unite principles thus separated, customs so excellent to craziness so strange, so ridiculous, and to principles so absurd?

The adepts must first start by confessing their past life and their sins to one of the leaders. Some [leaders] want them afterward to communicate it to the entire congregation of the perfect ones. After [*112*] formally renouncing the use of sex, and renouncing property, he is immediately admitted among them, and enters in the churches. The power of God is manifested in the twisting and in the gesticulations that they begin afterward to exercise, and the greater these signs are, the more often they are repeated, [the greater] indication of the advancement toward perfection, the more the divine Grace operates in them.

Such are their practices, such are their sentiments. Thus an obscure and uneducated woman, because of insanity, or vanity, has been able to add to the World the number of extravagances, and subsequently ornaments with a new trophy, the simulacre of Folly.

===

Of the Town of Udson.

===

From the valley of New Lebanon to pass to the Town of Udson there are counted about thirty-four miles, and one crosses continually small little hills. The road is passably kept, except for [*113*] the first miles at the exit of the valley; and the country that one goes through is not of the best [quality] and [is] sparsely inhabited. The homes of the farmers that one observes along the road give an appearance of great comfort. Four miles before arriving at Udson, one passes the village of Claverak, in which are seen some good homes; and a good building where the Courts are held.[96]

96. Claverack was the seat of the first courthouse of Columbia County.

The town of Udson is about four miles distant from the main road of N. York to Albany, and it is advantageously situated on the height of a promontory surrounded on three sides by the river of the same name. The surrounding countryside is on the plain and of an exceptional quality; but more excellent still is its location to be a seat of commerce. Four to five years ago Udson did not exist, and in the place where one counts today more than two hundred homes, there were but trees and forests. Some merchants understood the value of this place, made its purchase, and in two years there are counted already [114] more than eight hundred inhabitants. Because they are industrious, thus we can prophesy with certainty that Udson in little time will surpass Albany in richness and in population. The principal commerce that is practiced by its inhabitants is the export of grains and some quantity of salted meats. We saw in the shipyard there a cargo ship of about 150 tons.[97]

The town is built regularly, and the homes, a few excepted, are made of planks covered with bricks on the outside. They are for the most part built with elegance and neatness, and the poorest, those of the farmers and the artisans, are kept with much propriety.

We said above that Udson is built on an elevated promontory. The rock of this promontory upon which the town is built is composed of a black, hard, clayey stone, divisible in foliated layers, compact, and which in the cracks presents a rhomboid figure. [115] Exposed to the fire of the *chalumeau*[98] this stone decrepitated and with the borax and with the very fine salt fused, boiling into a dark-green glass. From these brief analyses we are induced to place this stone in the class of the schists, hard, clayey; even though at first sight we would have been induced to believe it a true trap rock. This rock is found in great regular banks tilted about 34° on the horizon from West to East. The banks of this stone are for the most part covered on the top by several feet of a brick-like shaped turf, which in some parts of the neighboring area composed by itself some great banks. The inhabitants make use of it, and besides manufacturing it for their own consumption they form a lucrative branch of export. The nearby hills provide also some good caves of limestone, of which we shall speak below.

---

97. Hudson was founded by Nantucket-born whale merchants and dealt primarily in beef, pork, fish, staves, oil, and candles, as well as the commodities mentioned by PA. Hudson became an authorized port of entry in 1790. Anna R. Bradbury, *History of the City of Hudson, New York* (Hudson, N.Y.: Record Printing and Publishing Company, 1908), 47–49.

98. Gas blow-lamp.

Exiting from the little town of Udson, and taking the New York road, one leaves on the right various hills, [*116*] of a calcareous nature, and there are found in this vicinity various lime kilns. This calcareous rock is of different [variable] quality; in some places of a greyish color, and in others whitish. The first one of these is of a fine and tight grain, and produces a limestone of good quality: the second of this variety is more compact, and susceptible to a mediocre cleaning. The banks of this one are generally superior to the greyish ones; and perfectly horizontal. When they fall naturally, they produce a cubic shape, which is seen clearly in the big blocks that one encounters in the vicinity of the road, right at the foot of the hills. At some hundred feet toward the South West the hills that are seen // they are also calcareous, but of a different nature than the two qualities heretofore mentioned. They are almost entirely composed of a mass of shells united by a calcareous juice. The banks of this nature continue in the vicinity of the river Udson for more miles beyond Albany.

[117]   Of West Point.

Under this denomination of West-point today is meant a point of land considerably advanced in the river Udson, at about fifty miles' distance from the City of New York, which was selected during the last war by the American army, as the opportune place where to erect a fortification to block the passage on the river, and the planned conjunction of the two English armies. In fact, examining this site carefully, and the circumstances of the time, we are convinced of the excellence of this position. Washington camped here with his army, and also made various stays at different times, but also when he was forced to take his army elsewhere, he left a strong detachment to maintain its possession. Today the fortifications are barely recognizable, and it would be otherwise difficult to recognize the previous location of the batteries, without [*118*] the help of a map, or of some eyewitness. The camp was surrounded by some external works, and these protected by two little forts each placed on opposite hills, which dominate the interior side, and would have impeded the enemy to attack this place from land in the event he would have tried it. In the arsenals there are found even today several cannons, but for the most part unusable. Today this fort is guarded by twenty men.

The hills on this side, which could be regarded as the basis of the Allegany [Mountains], are of primitive nature. We counted several varieties of granites, among which the most common is a rock with a quartzite base, with big knots of reddish feldspar, and bright mica. In the vicinity of these primitive rocks there have been found some piles of calamine stone. We did not have the opportunity to penetrate on this side.[99]

99. The journal ends here. A numbered page (119) without text follows.

Epilogue

"An Incredible Number of Enemies": The Betrayal of Paolo Andreani

Shortly after returning to New York, Paolo Andreani traveled to Philadelphia, where he spent the winter of 1790–91. His reason for going to Philadelphia was the removal of the national capital to that city. Late in the winter, however, the open and cordial hospitality he had enjoyed in New York turned into indifference and even hostility in the City of Brotherly Love. This change was the result of two incidents that illuminate the honor-consciousness of the capital and the informal but influential role elite women played in politics there. These incidents also bore out the prevalence of what Virginia governor Henry Lee described as "the servile custom of re-echoing whatever is communicated without respect to fact."[1]

The first incident stemmed from comments Andreani made at a jovial *convivium* of young members of the Philadelphia elite. As John Rutledge, Jr., related it from Andreani's retelling, a lively debate arose over the relative elegance of the ladies of England and their American counterparts.[2] Asked to pass judgment, Andreani "decreed in favour of the english ladies." While his decision was acclaimed by the "young John Bull" who had pressed England's case, it might not have had the same effect with many of the rest of those present, and Andreani incautiously added that "the French women were the most graceful he had ever known—that he had never known one who was not graceful & that <u>a French washerwoman</u> he thought infinitely more graceful than <u>an English lady of fashion</u>." Andreani's woes began when "some damned good natured friend" seized the opportunity to take the count down a peg. He embellished Andreani's statements by making the national hierarchy of female beauty more explicit and blunt and emphasizing that Andreani ranked his hostesses at the bottom.

1. Quoted in Joanne Freeman, *Affairs of Honor: National Politics in the New Republic* (New Haven, Conn.: Yale University Press, 2001), 66.
2. John Rutledge, Jr., to William Short, March 30, 1791, reel 23, William Short Papers, Library of Congress, Washington, D.C.

Since their city was now receiving refugees from the French Revolution, this was no idle challenge to the women of Philadelphia, and they responded accordingly.

Rutledge reported:

In a few hours it was known all over the City what Andriani had said. The Town was in an uproar & a convention of Ladies was called. The delinquent was charged with having made a criminal speech & . . . was sentenced to go into banishment. The Count was informed that in an assembly half of all the handsome & ugly Ladies in Philad[elphi]a it was unanimously resolved that in consequence of having made a speech containing libellous matter no lady present at the assembly should in future receive the visit of the said Count. No sentence to be sure could appear more dreadful to an italian than that which banished him from the company of the ladies.[3]

Convicted in absentia, Andreani appealed to the leaders of the assembly, "throwing himself at their feet & imploring forgiveness he might be again restored to Society." The results were uneven but satisfactory. Rutledge wrote, "The beautiful Mrs. B[ingham] Was too good a Christian not to forgive so repentant a sinner. She pitied & she pardoned him. She resuscitated his drooping spirits & promised that she would again admit him to her dining room." Bingham was doubtless an easy sell; Philadelphia's foremost *salonnière*, she had defended the virtues of elite French women to a skeptical Jefferson in 1787 and was an avid consumer of French clothes and skin products as well.[4]

The enactment of a mock trial with the distinctly democratic overtones of the "convention" and "assembly" by women with no legal standing independent of their husbands and fathers was simultaneously transgressive and conservative (but in effect mostly the latter). However, its political significance was magnified by a problem that flared not long after this one had subsided. Andreani's first intimation that his troubles were not at an end was a new "coldness" with which he was treated by President Washington. Friends soon informed Andreani that some comments attributed to him had been circulating through the capital. Unaware of the nature of these comments, Andreani was dismayed to learn they were a partial or corrupted excerpt from a July 1790 letter to Miranda in which he had mocked Adams and Jefferson

3. Rutledge to Short, March 30, 1791.
4. Anne Bingham to Jefferson, June 1, 1787, *Papers of Thomas Jefferson*, 11:392–94; Jefferson to Bingham, February 7, 1787, 11:122–24; Robert C. Alberts, *The Golden Voyage: The Life and Times of William Bingham* (Boston: Houghton Mifflin, 1969), 213–15; Susan Branson, *These Fiery Frenchified Dames: Women and Political Culture in Early National Philadelphia* (Philadelphia: University of Pennsylvania Press, 2001), 134–40. Henry Knox had recommended Andreani to William Bingham in a letter drafted July 6, 1790, reel 26, Henry Knox Papers, Massachusetts Historical Society, Boston.

and the republican court generally.[5] They had rebounded across the Atlantic in a confidential communication David Humphreys had sent to Washington from London.[6] Humphreys had been dispatched to Europe by Washington to perform the delicate task of gathering intelligence on the possible war between England and Spain. Humphreys reported that "everything here carries an aspect favorable to the credit & reputation of our Country." However, "there are accounts & descriptions of the state of public affairs transmitted from [America] to [England], which I little expected to find and which in my opinion may have a pernicious effect in fixing on the minds of men an erroneous idea of our real situation." In particular, he detailed his understanding of assertions made by Andreani in his letter to Miranda:

The Count Andriani has written things monstrously absurd & ill-founded: such in respect to their import as follow—that the United States are divided into two factions, Mr Jefferson and the northern States in favor of France, the southern States and New York in favor of Britain—that Congress had done nothing but quarrel about the seat of Government, and that this circumstance was what probably gave you the air of anxiety which he had remarked—that there was no man in Congress but Mr Madison who argued in a gentleman-like & solid manner—nor, in short, any man out of it in America but Colo. Hamilton, who possessed abilities: with a great deal of stuff about American parade & luxury not worth repeating. These idle tales, however, are propagated in such a manner as to be in danger of making unfavorable & false impressions.[7]

Washington replied to Humphreys by remarking that Andreani's comments "are such as do no credit to his judgment, and as little to his heart—They are the superficial observations of a few months residence, and an insult to the inhabitants of a country where he has received much more attention and civility than he seems to merit."[8] The historian Joanne Freeman notes that Washington had the letter circulated—a prime example of what she termed "the art of paper war," not to mention "evidence of Washington's oft-overlooked political savvy."[9] In fact, savvy shades into opportunism when we look more closely into the details. It was not Andreani's letter that Washington released to be "handed abroad" in a clandestine fashion but rather

5. Andreani to Miranda, July 8, 1790, Archivo del General Miranda 6:57–62.
6. David Humphreys to George Washington, October 31, 1790, *Papers of George Washington, Presidential Series*, 6:596–600.
7. Ibid., 6:597.
8. Washington to Humphreys, March 16, 1791, *Papers of George Washington, Presidential Series*, 7:583.
9. Freeman, *Affairs of Honor*, 216, 317 n. 17; Tobias Lear to Humphreys, March 16, 1791, Rosenbach Museum and Library, Philadelphia.

Humphreys' secondhand account. Once again, Andreani had found himself tried and convicted in absentia for comments attributed to him and embellished in the process. With "the Ladies all at war with" Andreani, Washington saw the opportunity to drive a perceived enemy from the capital, where he feared Andreani might have damaged the nation's reputation.[10] As an honor-conscious aristocrat, Andreani recognized that withdrawal was the only course.

In a letter to his brother, Andreani noted that the American envoy's report did not accurately reflect the complete content of his letter.[11] However, if Andreani developed ill will toward his American hosts, it was not so indiscriminate as to prevent him from requesting Gian Mario select "four of the best wheels of cheese" for him "to make a present of it to four or five families here." Clearly, Americans were not uniformly opposed to the count, even if he felt that he had inadvertently "created an incredible number of enemies."[12] The cheese—if it ever arrived—would have doubtless been enjoyed by the Binghams, for Washington's secretary informed Humphreys that Andreani "is still caressed by some—particularly Mr. & Mrs. Bingham & others who are fond of everything that does not belong to their own Country."[13]

How Humphreys obtained his passing knowledge of the letter's contents is not clear. Perhaps a close associate of Miranda told Humphreys what he knew, had read, or had heard of Andreani's troublesome letter. Or maybe Miranda had spoken aloud of it; Humphreys had characterized him as "an active, shrewd, studious, noisy man." What is certain is that Andreani had run afoul of a downside of the Republic of Letters: while there was honor and acclaim to be won through the circulation of one's opinions and observations through letters and journals, information was difficult to control, and the result could wreak havoc on one's reputation. He knew the risks of putting pen to paper, and his request for confidentiality bespoke the quasi-public nature of written communication in the eighteenth century.[14]

In retrospect, Andreani's estrangement from Philadelphia's highest social circles might have saved his life. Early in the spring of 1791, Andreani had requested permission to travel to the Ohio frontier with General Arthur St. Clair, who was to march that fall against the

10. Rutledge to Short, March 30, 1791.
11. Andreani to Gian Mario Andreani, April 7, 1791, FSA-ASMI.
12. Ibid.
13. Lear to Humphreys, March 16, 1791.
14. Dena Goodman, *The Republic of Letters* (Ithaca, N.Y.: Cornell University Press, 1994), 16–17, 139–52; Freeman, *Affairs of Honor*, 114.

hostile western confederacy nations allied under Miami chief Little
Turtle. Andreani was eager to see the far interior regions of America
and to "witness . . . a way of waging war totally different from ours."[15]
Andreani's request was denied, and he was forced to change his plans.
General St. Clair would suffer an even more disastrous defeat than
the one to which Andreani had referred in his letter; 600 of his 1,400-
man force were killed.

Still, Andreani had to leave Philadelphia. The social climate in the
capital had become too unpleasant for the controversial and unreli-
able Italian count. Even his scientific studies did not seem to proceed
smoothly. On May 14 Thomas Jefferson wrote Senator Thomas Sum-
ter the following message:

I am really mortified at the account I am obliged to give you of the fate of the
ores you confided to my care. I gave them you know to Count Andriani whose
regular chemical education, and his fondness for that study, together with his
leisure, induced me to expect an attentive and scientific analysis of them. I
enquired of him continually from time to time, and he always told me he was
trying them with solvents, and that the solution was going on. Being about to
take a journey myself, I sent two days ago to his lodgings to ask the result of
his experiments, or at least the prospect of the result. To my surprise my mes-
senger brought me word that he had left town on a long journey. I will certainly know on his return something definitive; but I confess to you I expect
he has failed of success in his trial of them.[16]

Andreani had silently decamped to New York and on May 15 he
departed on a sloop bound for Albany. He then proceeded by land to
Lake George, passed Lake Champlain, and on June 2 arrived in Montreal. After a trip along the entire course of the St. Lawrence, Andreani hurried back to that city. Thwarted in his earlier plan of a grand
voyage, he now hired a large birchbark canoe outfitted by the trading
company of Forsyth and Richardson. With a crew of a dozen *canadiens*, Andreani departed Montreal on July 1 and followed the Ottawa
River to Lake Nipissing. By way of the French River he entered Geor-
gian Bay, passed Manitoulin Island, and crossed Lake Huron to Fort
Michilimackinac, the British military and trading post situated at the
entrance to Lake Michigan. Here he rested and took on supplies before departing on the next leg of this long voyage. Passing Sault Ste.
Marie into the *Gitchi Gumi*, Andreani navigated counterclockwise
across Lake Superior all the way to present-day Minnesota. He gathered

15. Paolo Andreani to Gian Mario Andreani, April 7, 1791.
16. *Papers of Thomas Jefferson*, 20:410–11.

information on the fur trade, later published by La Rochefoucauld in his 1799 *Travels Through the United States.*[17] In September of 1791 Andreani reached La Pointe on Madeleine Island off the coast of Wisconsin, where he met the trader John Johnston, who later recounted his encounter with an Italian nobleman intent on taking measurements of the curvature of the Earth.[18] Andreani made it back to Montreal that fall via Detroit and Lake Erie.

Andreani eventually returned to the sufficiently good graces of Philadelphians that he was elected member number 566 of the American Philosophical Society before returning to Europe in June of 1792. He arrived in Portsmouth, England, on July 14, where he wrote his brother of his "wretched" finances.[19] Andreani resided in London until 1794, when he was finally able to return to Milan. But the departure of the Austrians and the arrival of Napoleon Bonaparte in 1796 placed an additional burden on Count Paolo's precarious finances. He criticized the new taxes imposed upon the Milanese nobility in his frequent correspondence with Gian Mario, who had meanwhile relocated with his wife to a country estate to avoid the tumults of the time. In order to avoid his creditors, Paolo eventually left Milan and began traveling again thanks to additional help from his brother. From the numerous letters Paolo wrote Gian Mario in those years and the several passports he secured, we learn that between the end of 1796 and the end of 1806 the count traveled throughout Italy, France, and England before once again crossing the Atlantic.

Andreani's second voyage to the Americas began in the fall of 1806 and was recorded in a series of diaries, some of which have survived. In the first, a fifty-four-page notebook, he recounted the long Atlantic crossing and the unscheduled landing in Jamaica forced by a British schooner upon the French vessel on which he traveled.[20] In Kingston, Andreani witnessed the "horrible slave trade." He was eventually able to secure a passage to New Orleans, his original destination, where he arrived in February 1807. He had, however, contracted smallpox. The assistance of a fellow Milanese who lived in New Orleans saved Andreani from being placed in quarantine by the authorities and helped his recovery. In the spring of 1808, while still convalescing in New Orleans, Andreani sent a warm letter in French to James Madison, then secretary of state under Thomas Jefferson. He expressed his desire "to renew

17. Andreani, "Accounts of the Fur Trade, extracted from the Journal of Count Andriani, of Milan, who travelled in the interior parts of America in the Year 1791," *Thirteenth Report of the Bureau of Archives for the Province of Ontario* (1916): 110–16.

18. Henry Rowe Schoolcraft, *Oneóta, or Characteristics of the Red Race of America* (New York: Wiley and Putnam, 1845), 299–301.

19. Paolo Andreani to Gian Mario Andreani, July 14, 1792, FSA-ASMI.

20. Andreani, *Viaggio in Nord America*, ed. Fortunato, 53–98.

with you my dear sir the connection that the political events of Europe interrupted for a long span of years." He also informed Madison of his intention to visit their common friend Benjamin Rush in Philadelphia to seek his medical advice regarding his poor health.[21] Andreani visited Florida in September of that year.[22]

The following year he reached Georgetown and the infant city of Washington. Andreani's reaction to the latter was unequivocally negative. In his diary titled *Of Georgetown, and in addition the plan for the city of Washington 1809,* the Italian count gave the city planners and its architects a lashing.[23] He attacked Pierre Charles L'Enfant for the "illogical" and "irregular" layout of the city, aping Versailles. He then vilified his old acquaintance William Thornton for his original work on the Capitol, which Andreani described as "bizarre, without talent, without art, and without taste." He also condemned Benjamin Latrobe as "a bricklayer transformed into an architect and the director of a vast monument [the Capitol] that will perpetuate the memory of the barbaric taste of this nation for the *belle arti.*" Nor was he pleased with Thomas Jefferson for the "Frenchness" evident in the effort to replicate the architecture of Paris in the capital. Echoing the infamous letter to Miranda, Andreani called the United States a nation "full of vainglory" and its citizens "a new people, uneducated." Andreani also visited Philadelphia and Baltimore, where he tersely noted the rapid growth of those cities and New York since the time of his first voyage to America in 1790.[24]

Between 1809 and 1811 Andreani visited Cuba and several other islands in the Greater and Lesser Antilles, including Curaçao, Grenada, and Barbados. After a brief return to the United States, he sailed to Martinique and St. Thomas. In early 1812 Andreani was finally back in Europe. His unsettled life and the impossibility of returning to Milan, where he was sought for his debts, forced him to wander from Lisbon to London, then south to Cadiz in Spain, to seek a climate more suitable to his deteriorating physical condition.[25] In 1817 Andreani finally settled in salubrious Nice, where he lived quite modestly and largely forgotten by his friends and peers. Some months before his sixtieth birthday, Andreani received the sad news of the death of his sister Cecca, a premonition perhaps that he was soon to follow. Bedridden as a result of a degenerative gout, Count Paolo Andreani died in the early morning of May 11, 1823.

21. Andreani to James Madison, March 8, 1808, James Madison Papers, Library of Congress, Washington, D.C. This letter is erroneously indexed under May 11.

22. Andreani made only a brief notation of this trip. Fortunato, ed., *Viaggio,* 99–102.

23. Ibid., 103–21.

24. Ibid., 123–28.

25. Dicorato, *Paolo Andreani,* 228, 265–82.

Appendix
Selected Letters, 1790–1791

*Unless otherwise noted, all letters are from the Fondo Sormani-Andreani, Archivio di
Stato, Milan, Italy, and translated from the Italian by Cesare Marino.*

To GIAN MARIO ANDREANI

C[aro].F[ratello]. [Dear Brother]
Halifax in Nova Scotia
26 May 1790

Ten days ago I wrote to You from the sea with the opportunity of the
vessel Robert, of Capt. Houper[?], with whom we met for a few hours,
and even though I do not have anything new or important to tell You,
today nonetheless I do not let pass the opportunity of a vessel departing for England without giving You my news. We arrived here this
morning always pushed by the fresh and strong winds for the forty-
four days that the voyage lasted, and we are only waiting for the dis-
patches of the Governor[1] to continue for New York. As my plan is to
visit Canada, I was very disappointed I was unable to accept the offer
made to me this morning by Admiral Hughes[2] to take me on board
his fleet to Quebec, but since I did not have letters of credit for any
merchants in those parts, thus I lost a unique opportunity. In twenty
hours one can say nothing of a country; nonetheless, the surroundings of this Capital are exceedingly savage and there is neither population nor vegetation. A few days ago arrived here five Indian Chiefs
of the nations that border the Mississippi,[3] and they intend to continue
their voyage until London, to beg for the protection of that court

1. Governor John Parr (1725–91).
2. Sir Richard Hughes (1729–1812), naval commander-in-chief for eastern British
North America.
3. According to a letter written by the leader of the delegation, Tory William Augus-
tus Bowles, the Cherokees were Unatoy, Kuahtekiske; the Creeks were Seponejah,
Tuskeniah, and Wosseo (Moses Price). "The Representation of William Augustus
Bowles . . . to His Britannic Majesty," January 3, 1791, Public Records Office, F.O. L/9,
S/J.9756, fols. 5–17, London.

against the Spaniards. I had lunch with them today at the Governor's, and as they speak a little Spanish thus I could converse with them. The portrait they paint of the oppression they suffer is truly frightening. One thousandth of the truth in their story would today reflect on Spain with horror. From New York I will give You my news, and perhaps I would have then material to write. Please give my dear greetings to the Contessina[4] and to all the friends, and believe me

Your most aff. obed. Brother Paolo

To Gian Mario Andreani

New York 7. July 1790.

C.F.

It is with the greatest regret that I find myself without Your latest news with the royal Dispatch which arrived a few days ago from England, and which departed five weeks after me from Falmouth. And yet I instructed Mr. Battier Zorlin [?] to check at the Post office in London whether there were any letters addressed to me and to mail them, therefore I doubt there were any in reality. We here are awaiting another vessel momentarily, and I hope to find some; hoping at the same time that You have received my two which I wrote to you, one from Nova Scotia, and the other one a few days earlier from the sea.—From Halifax to this harbor I had a navigation of about 14 days, but of favorable and pleasant winds; and here I find myself in the midst of good people who love foreigners, and whom they receive with hospitality. It was my first idea to spend the coming winter in this City; but because the Congress and the President Wasington are moving soon to Philadelphia, thus I will change my mind and I too shall transfer to that City, to winter there.

The news arrived here of an unavoidable break between England and Spain has already made a great sensation in this country, where the more shrewd ones see from this very moment what will be the difficulty of coming out of it with honor and profit. In fact, this country in its present state finds itself in the most critical circumstances, having neither credit, nor easy means to pay the interest on the national debt, without turning to onerous taxes on its people. To all of these internal embarrassments is added now the impossibility, I

---

4. Countess Fulvia Visconti (d. 1824), wife of Gian Mario.

would say, of making sure its flag is respected, not having a single armed vessel; and to prevent some merchants from arming under the British flag, and moving against the Spanish settlements, to use the analogy of the [English] language, which could induce Spain to ask for satisfaction. If I were to give faith to the news that here spreads at every moment, I should believe that the whole of Europe is in flames; but the news from the sea merits double confirmation than that in the gazettes. Even of the poor Pope we hear a lot here, and it is said he was assassinated by the Cagliostrani;[5] and that our own Milan united with another state in Italy in open uprising. As for myself, I believe there are some bad [happenings], but not so black as they are portrayed. Nonetheless, I await the news from Europe with impatience, and I await for Yours also regarding more interesting matters, for everything that concerns Your health and that of the Contessina, whom I beg you to greet on my behalf, together with all the friends, among whom Your D. Santino. I embrace you, and I am

Your most aff. obed. B.[rother] Paolo

To Francisco de Miranda[6]

N. York 8 July 1790

I seize with urgency the first opportunity which presents itself to send you my news, and that of all your loyal Friends here. I will not convey anything to you about my passage, having already painted a disagreeable picture of it in a letter I wrote to General Melville[7] from Halifax, and which he has probably passed on to you. Besides, why waste one's time describing storms, annoyances, and dangers of all kinds, when one can say, I have arrived and I am in good health! That is all we owe our Friends, *et tantum Catis* for this.—As I propose to bore you with a long letter, I will leave out nothing of all I have done, all I have seen, and all I plan to do and see. I recall that you missed seeing Nova Scotia; but on this point I can reassure you, since I will be so bold as to say that it does not merit investigation by a man such as yourself. In

5. Followers of Count Alessandro di Cagliostro, actually Giuseppe Balsamo (1743–1795), a Sicilian confidence artist and Freemason.
6. *Archivo del General Miranda*, 6: 57–62. Translated from the French by CM and KMT.
7. Robert Melville (1723–1809) was a brigadier general and former governor-in-chief of the British West Indies, where he founded the Royal Botanic Garden on the island of St. Vincent.

the short period of time that I spent in its Capital and its environs, I formed a very unfavorable opinion of that settlement, and I think Mr. Wilkes was quite correct to say in one of his memorable discourses, *but I had almost forgot that we still possess the little fishing hamlet of Halifax.*[8] When I compare the coast of Nova Scotia with the beautiful surroundings of this city, I can only lament the fate of the royalists, who were obliged to emigrate. A wonderful lesson for all who support the ambitious and despotic views of Kings! The city of Halifax is well enough situated on the slope of a hill, and built regularly and neatly, although the houses are all of wood. It is not fortified, except by a few old earthworks in very poor condition and not in a state of readiness. The port is one of the most attractive and secure I know, forming a very nice shoreline, in the middle of which is a fortified island, [but if ships] can anchor safely below, the fortifications of this island will be useless. The land which surrounds the port and its long bay is completely barren; and it is only with all the skill and patience of its cultivators that we see today a little greenery. Rocks stick out in every direction to thwart labor, and they are an insurmountable obstacle. During my stay I traveled a few miles into the interior and I must admit I never saw anything more barren, more sad, more savage. On top of all the problems of the land, the inhabitants suffer that of the climate. The winter is very long and harsh, and summer brings dense fogs which make the atmosphere very humid; The interior of the province is of a different condition, if I am to believe the Governor's account. There the land is fertile, and produces everything one would want; but the fact is that Halifax imports from Boston and other New England ports all its provisions, be it meat, vegetables, or some of its wheat, that are needed for its inhabitants. Fish is a great bargain: but by contrast everything else is extraordinarily expensive. The Captain of the vessel bought chickens to take on board, and he paid five English shillings each for them. That's just an example.—It was in this city that I saw and spoke with five Indian chiefs, three Cheerikes [Cherokees] and two Creeks. They complain about the Spanish government and they paint a horrible picture of its rule. They request the protection of England to chase the tyrants from the two Floridas, and perhaps while they are traveling preparations are under way for an event in Europe that will be favorable to their views. I speak, my friend, of the threat of war of which we were informed a few days ago, and which surprised us all.[9] In truth I would have expected anything to happen

8. In English in original.
9. The Nootka Sound controversy was sparked by the Spanish seizure of British trade vessels in the Pacific.

but this, since I do not believe that Spain is capable of facing up to England's maritime power, nor protecting its colonies and domains in America. Perhaps the moment has arrived for mankind to find happiness, and South America can move quickly from a state of oppression and barbarism to the liberty and happiness that nature marked out for it. The greatest events now take place with such ease and rapidity that nothing is impossible any longer. But I am too far from the stage on which these grand Operas are being performed to add anything else. On the contrary, I urgently await your news, and your reflections. Let us turn to N. York.

The view of New York Bay seemed just as you described it to me, and after having visited Long Island and the field of the first battle, even I the most ignorant of men in military matters, I am convinced that if a *general* had cut down the tree of independence on that day, the efforts of the American colonies who rebelled against the nation would have made a very faint appearance in English history. But happily Howe[10] commanded one side and Washington the other. Patience and dexterity on one side and poor judgment on the other saved this great cause, and the seed of what is taking place among us in Europe. They say the construction of this city has greatly improved, and in truth there are new houses that look quite attractive and are built with elegance. But taste is lacking altogether in anything that concerns architecture. A new church was just built in bad gothic taste, and it is admired by everyone—But let us turn from the buildings to something more interesting. Your letters were frankly the most useful to me, since they enabled me to make the acquaintance of the most learned and honest men, while those of others introduced me to rather prejudiced persons resembling the corrupt Europeans of the great cities. What I am about to add will be just between us; because, as my visit has only been very short, I may very well have been mistaken in a hasty judgment. Hamilton, Knox,[11] Duar,[12] etc. received me with kindness and they are all the best men in the world, ready to be of service and help a stranger. W. S. Smith[13] I have only seen once and Liwingston[14] is in the countryside. Hamilton showed me a financial plan that I read with pleasure (and which I will send you at the first opportunity) containing some splendid financier's insights, and a good deal of

10. General William Howe (1729–1814).
11. General Henry Knox (1750–1806) was secretary of war.
12. William Duer (1747–99) had stepped down as assistant secretary of the treasury in February.
13. William Stephens Smith (1755–1816), U.S. marshal of the district of New York. Smith had traveled with Miranda in Europe in 1785.
14. Robert R. Livingston (1746–1813).

justice. In this essay the learned men who have a share in the government believed they perceived ambition and they united to disparage
it; although I am of the opinion that it must needs play a role in one
manner or another.

Knox was not any more successful in his military project; and in
truth he did not have a foundation good enough to support it. Also
he did not find anyone else who supported it; even though nobody
substituted a better one or even one at all. Duar who left (as you know)
his position of secretary of the finance ministry, for the enterprise of
the new colonies on the Ohio, has not yet made his fortune; but I
believe that he preaches for the right cause, and that he will finish by
seeing his project crowned [with success] and his purse filled.[15] Smith
Marshal supports the party of his father-in-law,[16] and he does not occupy himself with anything else; at least that is what I have been told.
I lunched with Mr. Adams with him; we spoke of you all the time and
I hope to induce him to send you the journal as soon as it is copied.—
Hamilton is very oppressed by everyone, and among his greatest enemies are Jefferson and Madison with whom I find myself lodged at
Mrs. Elsworth's. The first of these two works against Hamilton in the
government, and the second uses his eloquence openly in Congress to
the same end, and unfortunately they are both held in high esteem by
the public, and are very dominant. But Jefferson it appears to me that
he brought from Europe everything bad that he saw there, and very
little of what exists there of good: thus he is proud of his position as
Secretary of foreign affairs, as much as Kaunitz in Vienna, and with
regard to hospitality it seems he does not remember that he is Virginian. Madison stripped of his political harassments is a man of merit.
He is a good orator and has a great number of philosophical views in
all areas: he is perhaps the most educated man that I have met here;
and I think he aspires to become the minister in Paris replacing his
friend and idol Jefferson. I would like to paint you a picture of Washington, if I could claim to have known him. The first time that I visited him, I had that veneration for him that I will have my whole life;
and that day he interested me more than since. On that occasion he
was alone in his room and not surrounded by anyone, except by his
glory and his name; and the other times I found him in the middle of
the pomp of a Court, which, though miserable, dare I say ridiculous,

15. Duer was a principal in the Scioto Land Company, which attracted many émigrés
from France but was ultimately unable to meet its commitment to settle them at Gallipolis. As a result of the failure of this and other financial schemes, Duer was consigned to debtor's prison in 1792.

16. William Stephens Smith was John Adams's son-in-law.

is nonetheless a Court. In this respect, my dear Miranda, things have changed since your visit, and changed rapidly, and what is worse not for the better. Washington opposed it for as long as he could; but he had to give way to public feeling, and have levees in form; and be eternally surrounded by four good aides de camp, and I do not know how many Secretaries. The levee is once per week at 3 o'clock in the afternoon, for the convenience of the members of Congress; and there the President of the United States sees the world like the King at St. James, says a word to all boredom an hour, and he plants there those who do not plant him first. What is more extraordinary, he and the whole court is in complete costume with sword, while the visitors are in formal dress; but with hairstyles and shoes like the dandies in London or Paris, to say the least. The simplicity that reigned here before and that is so necessary for a new country, poor, indebted, and without credit, is banished from the homes, and from almost all the cities of the United States. Some trustworthy People assure me that Philadelphia is unrecognizable; that luxury is excessive because [people have] means, and that bankruptcies are very frequent. A certain Bingham[17] lives there like a prince in Europe, while one is not sure of his fortune, because he had a fifty thousand pound St[erlin]g house built without having paid anyone. Here, except in two or three instances, I have dined with all European formality; and I have not yet been invited to share a family dinner which pleases me as much and charms a foreigner. It is said that those who live in the countryside have conserved the former usage; but I fear that the style will spread everywhere, since in Virginia where hospitality was the rule, one begins to have a need for inns, and a great number are being built there. Vice President Adams is the most pompous man I know and the most selfish that exists. What are they doing in France? he said to me the other day; I believe that they are madmen and that they did not understand my work. Well I'll go there myself and explain it to them.[18] What do you say, you my dear friend, of this beginning? God prevent his becoming President! the country would change faces in little time. A few days ago I lunched with him and Mr. Washington. That day I was surprised to see the President of the United States arrive at a private lunch with such formality. He was alone with his wife in a six horse coach with

17. William Bingham (1752–1804), Federalist senator from Pennsylvania.

18. According to Louis-Guillaume Otto, the French chargé d'affaires in America, "[Adams] told me one day with his customary modesty: 'I see well that I will have to make another trip to France in order to explain to them my book which they have not rightly understood.'" The book in question was Adams's *Discourses on Davila.* Margaret M. O'Dwyer, ed. and trans., "A French Diplomat's View of Congress, 1790," *William and Mary Quarterly*, 3rd ser. 21 (1964): 433.

glass panes, preceded by two postillions on horseback and followed by two Aides de Camp also on horseback, and two in a reserve coach. What do you say my Friend of this procession which is unknown to you?—The Congress has almost completed the current session without deciding anything important; and the members have neglected the finance affairs for debates on the location to choose as an interim residence for Congress—After much imbroglio it seems that today Philadelphia has won; but as one must debate the question again in Congress, one is not quite certain of the outcome of this affair.—

I was more fortunate in my philosophical research. I arrived only a few days ago, and already I have gathered different stones unknown in Europe; and observed a few new facts of physics. With such a proportion the troubles and the pains of my journey will be paid with a large interest. In two or three days I intend to go to Albany, and to go to Philadelphia crossing New Jersey. Those are my plans dear Friend. I beg you to excuse this very long letter. When you see General Melvill give him my compliments, and wish him good health from me, which is all that is needed for a man of his merit. Conserve your own; and remember that across the ocean is Your very affectionate Friend and humble servant.

Andreani
P. S. Col. de Miranda

to the Care of Daniel Parker Esqr.
N° 2. Leisterfield—Square

London.

To Gian Mario Andreani

Philadelphia 30 January 1791

C.F.
With the courier vessel of November which has since departed four days ago, I received Your dearest of the 16th of October, and to my great surprise I find myself deprived of news by the arrival of the vessel of December, which having had a shorter crossing arrived only two days after the other one. For what reason, Dearest G. Mario, have you been able to remain silent for an entire month, particularly since I do not let pass any opportunity without writing to You? I want to believe that your letters were lost, rather than presume another reason. This letter I hope will reach to you in double, as I am sending one by the

ordinary way of England, and a copy by the French channel. I was induced to do this by two reasons, the 1ˢᵗ by the hope that at least one of the two would reach you, and the 2ⁿᵈ by choosing two different ways I would not miss the shortest one. I wrote to You already several times that the credit given to me by Mr. Battier Zorlin Al.[?], was limited to the next month of February, hence the day after tomorrow I would have found myself almost without a *soldo*,[19] if during this time I had not saved about one hundred English pounds. Far away from You some five thousand miles, forced to wait for a response five or six months, I let You consider whether I should not be distressed by the consequences of a longer delay, above all since no mention at all was made in Your latest one. According to the usual calculation we should expect the next vessel in about fifteen days and I assure you that if with this new occasion I would find myself deprived of Your latest news, and missing the letter of credit, I would really be distressed.

My plan was to depart from here for Canada next month, the season being the most opportune for a trip of one thousand miles, for the reason that one can cross with ease on the ice all those immense lakes that delay travel in the summer. But in order to do so, I would have had already to procure the necessary passports to enter the English domains, which I cannot do without having a certain security. I will say no more on this subject, having said enough writing to you.

Please congratulate Yourself on my behalf with Cav[alier]. Castiglioni for the publication of his viaggio,[20] and You please do me the favor of sending me a copy with the utmost diligence, it being infinitely more pleasureable and advantageous to read such work in the very place about which it reasons. By the route of Genoa I suppose there will be good opportunities. Greet on my behalf the Contessina, and assure Her of all my esteem and affection; similarly to the friends, and You believe me

Your most obed. aff. Brother Paolo

P.S. In the last few days I had a rather violent attack of fever which I attribute to the extraordinary change of climate that one experiences here almost every day. Today I feel much better.[21]

19. An Italian coin, i.e., "penniless."
20. Luigi Castiglioni, *Viaggio negli Stati Uniti dell'America settentrionale fatto nel 1785, 1786 e 1787,* 2 vols. (Milan: Giuseppe Marelli, 1790).
21. William Shippen (1736–1808), M.D., registered a visit from Andreani on January 24. William Shippen, Jr., prescription book, American Philosophical Society Library, Philadelphia.

To Gian Mario Andreani

Philadelphia, the 7th April 1791

C.F.

Your dearest of the 21st of December did not get to me until last night, the courier vessel having had a very long crossing. I thank You for the credit letter that You favored me with, and I will say nothing more on this matter. Mr. Battier has sent me here one for £. 1800 instead of the two thousand, thus keeping the sum of two hundred *lire*, he having paid £162.15. s., part as a deposit, // whose cost amounts to double of what I had written You, and of what I had figured out // and for some clothing I ordered when I was in Dublin. Now that the credit note has arrived I will start traveling, and I have resolved to give You an idea, so that You may follow me on the map.

From here crossing for more than 300 m[iles]. the State of Pennsylvania I will arrive at Fort Pitt, and from there descending the River Ohio and the Mississippi I will visit New Orleans. During the long navigation of these two rivers / about 2000 miles // I will stop sometime to observe the new French establishments formed by the emigrants of the last two years,[22] and the country of Kentucky that will form in a few months a separate State. Such a voyage requires today prudence and circumspection, not just for the dangers of the navigation in the deserted countries that one travels through, but rather because of the cruel war that exists for already one year between the United States and the various nations of Indians. The troops sent last year were defeated with great losses, and this year the States have voted for an army of four thousand men. I will follow the troops, and I will obtain therefore the pleasure of traveling more cautiously, and to be a witness to a mode of warfare altogether different from our own.

A few weeks ago I had the displeasure of seeing here circulate publicly an alleged letter of mine written to a friend in London. The long paragraph transmitted was not, in fact, that which I wrote, and in part loaded; but because in it I spoke freely of the ministers, and of various people involved in the government, and most of all I attacked the gentle sex, therefore I have, without wanting it, created an incredible number of enemies. Nonetheless I did not say but half of what, if I live, I will say one day. The best is to hurry up to see the country, and return to the motherland.

The news of the privileges obtained by our country reached me

22. The ill-fated Gallipolis colony, promoted by Duer's Scioto Land Company.

here from Vienna, and from Paris, already more than a month ago, and consoled me indeed. I wish to Heaven that such a signaled advantage may be stable, and sufficient to heal our poor country. Greet on my behalf affectionately the Contessina, and thus as well all the friends, and the good Ab[bot?] Calvi who does not write to me anymore. I embrace You tenderly and I subscribe myself

of Yours most obed. aff. Brother Paolo

P.S. I wish good luck to this leaf, and may Heaven make it reach N. York in time to be sent with the vessel that must depart in the morning. The courier had brought the most distressing news from the sea. In a very violent storm were lost at sea several vessels that departed from here in December, and most of all [one] on which I had sent you a case with minerals and other natural curiosities, with various letters.

To Gian Mario Andreani

Philadelphia, the 7th April 1791

C.F.

After I wrote the leaf of today, and mailed it, I remembered I had forgotten to beg you for a favor. There are some friends of mine here who have often heard spoken about our cheese from Lodi, without ever tasting it, hence I wish to make a gift of it to some four or five families. Do me therefore the favor, D[ear] Brother, to have someone choose four of the best wheels and to ship them to Genoa to Mr. Longhi with word to have them sealed with lead, and shipped to Cadiz, where there are often departures for this harbor. The below indicated direction will suffice. I beg You to give the order immediately, so that they may be here before the ice of next winter, which closes the navigation at the beginning of December.

I embrace You and I am __

of Yours most obed. aff. Brother Paolo

P.S.

To the care of Mr.
J. Vaughan, Merchant at
Philadelphia[23]

---

23. John Vaughan (1756–1841) was a prominent wine merchant, secretary of the American Philosophical Society, and president of the Philadelphia Society for the Promotion of Agriculture.

To Francisco de Miranda[24]

Philadelphia 7. April 1791

My Dear Friend:

After three months of silence, I find myself forced to importune you, despite being owed a response to the very long letter that I wrote you during the month of November,[25] and sent in December from this port by the ship *Washington*. The purpose of this letter, my friend, is to recount to you what has happened to me most recently on a subject that concerns you.—Two months ago the President of the United States, by showing me coldness, gave me suspicions that he had something against me. Not knowing what to apprehend, imagine my surprise, when a few days later my friends came to tell me that a paragraph from one of my letters had been sent to the Government by Colonel Humphries[26] (then in London) & by General Washington sent to different houses to be read. Not knowing the nature of that paragraph, I began to suspect that it was some literary frivolity, until by further research I came to the knowledge that it was what I confidentially communicated to you in a letter from last July. No cause for concern if it had been copied correctly, but, my dear friend, what I had written had been so badly represented that my own self-respect suffers from it as much as my peace of mind. Please, my dear friend do not show the letter from November; all that is there is of the most scrupulous truth according to my way of seeing; but since I shall have to spend some time in this country, it could damage me a lot. I wrote you as a friend, treat me accordingly, the paragraph in question has done me irreparable harm. The influential people, in general those attached to the President, everyone has become alarmed, and I do not have two people who view me favorably in the entire city.—I cannot conceive by what chance Mr. Humphries had knowledge of this letter, and I beseech you to explain it to me at the first opportunity. Colonel Smith,[27] who has been in London for several months, will have responded to you in person with regard to your papers, never having done it with me, after having received me with the greatest indifference. I have been told here that he is not one of your friends; you must learn more of this and be better informed.

24. *Archivo del General Miranda,* 6:106–8. Translated from the French by CM and KMT.
  25. Letter not found. It is likely PA was referring to the July 8 letter.
  26. David Humphreys (1752–1818).
  27. William Stephens Smith. He was in England to sell lands in upstate New York.

For my part I intend in a few days to go to the Ohio and descend by that river to the Mississipi, & from there to N. Orleans, if M. M. the Spaniards will permit me. During this voyage I will stop and see the new settlements of the French refugees on the Scioto River, & the new State of Kentucky. My friends would like to keep me from making this journey because of the danger of being captured by the Indians who are already molested, even though the season does not yet favor their depredations. General Sinclair[28] this year commands an army of four thousand men with the task of recouping the losses of the last campaign in which the troops under the orders of General Harmar[29] were beaten, and lost two hundred men. It is a bloody war, & so many do not believe that they will manage to end it in this campaign, since the regiments will not be ready to leave for another two months.—Colonel Hamilton triumphed in this past session over the entire cabal against his genius, and everything he proposed was passed. If the finances continue to be administered by a subject like him, the power of this country will soon be respectable beyond its population. Give my compliments to Gl. Melvill, and believe me, your best friend & Ob. St.

To Gian Mario Andreani

Philadelphia the 2nd May 1791

C.F.
Some rains that we have had here for several consecutive days have delayed my travels, having delayed the arrival of the letters from Canada, and the passport I requested a few months ago of the Governor of that province. Now I am ready for the march, and in the morning I will start in the direction of Quebec, in part by land and in greater part by water. The distance from this city to the capital of that province is about eight hundred miles, and it will take me a good month to arrive there. In Quebec I think I will make a brief stop, and travel to see the famous Cataract of Niagara, and the Lake Superior. This voyage will take the entire summer, and I do not know whether in the next Autumn I will be able to be at Terra Nuova[30] according to plans.

Here is in brief the plan for this year, and due to the distance of the places, and their remote location, it will not be easy from now on to write to You often, neither equally to receive Your letters regularly. Today I had to give a check of 150 pounds for reason of the long voyage, and

28. General Arthur St. Clair (1736–1818).
29. General Josiah Harmar (1753–1813).
30. Newfoundland.

of two horses that I had to purchase, one for the baggage, and another to replace one that died in the winter. Good thing, however, that they are not here as expensive as in the southern parts of this Continent.

The news that You sent me with Your last one regarding all that H[is] M[ajesty] has accorded to our country has filled me with consolation. I assure you that even though I have been far away from the motherland already a number of years, I am nonetheless a good patriot, and without a joke I would not not change my country if not for a very few ones; there aren=t perhaps but two that would compare with it. Nonetheless I believe that the graces obtained may not be sufficient to [promote] the perfect happiness of the country, and without annual representation, and the freedom to reject the extraordinary taxations, what is all the rest worth? But someone will tell me a little is better than nothing, and I subscribe to it.

I await here with impatience a copy of the viaggio of our Friend the Cav. Castiglioni that I already asked You for, as well as the news regarding the different qualities of terraces, etc. I will be grateful to You for letting me know by which means they will be delivered to me.

We are here definitely ignorant of what is happening in Europe. The news arrives tardily, and by the very deceitful channel of the English gazettes, which even our good D. Santino would not dare believe. These people do not really care much about the embarrassments of distant nations, whose existence is here known only by reason of some commercial link. The interests of this nation are rapidly rising. At the time of my arrival in June past, the public bonds were at 4½ on the *lira* [pound], and they are today at 17¾. The Dutch who have made here immense speculations have earned immense sums. This much can do the idea of a good constitution, and the ability truly extraordinary of the minister of finances Mr. Hamilton___

If you have money to invest there would not be anything better than to purchase some stocks in the national bank that will be set up in a few months. The seven percent is never lacking as ordinary interest, and one can naturally anticipate a better benefit. The security is such that I would put in it to my last *soldo*, if I had cash money.

Greet, I beg You, on my behalf the Contessina, and beg Her to write to me in Her own hand a few lines. Remember me to all the friends, and thank them for remembering me. You I embrace cordially, and remember I am grateful for all of Your favors.
Farewell.

Your most aff. obed. B. Paolo

To GIAN MARIO ANDREANI

New York the 9th May 1791

C.F.
This moment I arrived in this city and in a few minutes I will depart
for Albany, taking the opportunity of a vessel that sails for that city.
Even though there is not here a ready opportunity to mail this [letter
of] mine, nonetheless I will entrust it to a merchant with the task of
mailing it with the first vessel that will depart for England. The primary objective it is to obey to Your order that You have given me in
Your last one, to give You regular notice of all the drafts. The day 6 of
this month, a moment before leaving Philadelphia, I had to give another order of £.60 St[erling] to Mr. Vaughan for a letter of change
[credit] I will cash in a village on Lake Champlain, he not having been
able to give me a credit receipt, which I would have much preferred,
both for the embarrassment of carrying too much money in cash, and
for not increasing the withdrawals at the same time. I will procure to
be on the lookout for all the occasions that will be presented to me to
send You my news, but Your letters God knows when they will reach
me. Greet the Contessina dearly, and remember me to the friends. I
embrace You dearly, and I am Your most aff. obed. B. Paolo

To GIAN MARIO ANDREANI

Montreal 30 June 1791

C.F.
After my departure from Philadelphia I have traveled constantly, And
I have visited this English colony to the extremity of the Gulf of St.
Laurence. At Quebec I made a brief stay for the reason that the season was already well advanced, and not to waste time to execute the
entire plan I formulated for this year, that is to visit the interior parts
of Canada, at least to the one hundredth degree of Western longitude
from London. To this effect, I will depart from here tomorrow in a
Canoe armed [outfitted], and I will enter Lake Superior following the
River Ottawa. This voyage of many thousands of miles, and through a
country completely savage [wild], will not fail to be hard, and with
some difficulties: but since the Government has here given to me all
of the possible facilitations, and recommends me to the various chiefs
of the Indian nations, thus I hope to be able to accomplish my vast
plan without any accidents, and to be back in November.

The merchant to whom I was here directed has provided me with the canoe as well as the provisions for me, my servants, and eleven Canadiens, that form a small crew, and he asks me a letter [payment] for one hundred-fifty lire [pounds] that will be given in advance.

I have not had Your news already for four months, and I will not be able to have them for another five, which I leave it up to You to consider, if it should not be painful to me. I hope nonetheless that Your health and that of the Contessina be that which I hope with my heart, excellent. I send You no news, because here there is none that would interest a European. The only one that gives here a lot to think and to talk about is the fervor with which the Indian nations that inhabit the northern banks of the Ohio [River] are making preparations to attack the army that the United States are sending against them. At any moment we can expect the news of some bloody days. Greet the Contessina. I embrace You and I am

Your most aff. obed. Brother Paolo

Index

Page numbers in italics refer to illustrations.

Adams, John, 14, 91, 102, 103
agriculture, 20, 36, 42, 43, 50–54, 74, 77, 81, 87, 100. *See also* Iroquois
Albany, 18–19, 43–48, 111
Albany Dutch, 19, 22, 30, 45–46
Albany Pine Bush, 2, 48–49
Alfieri, Vittorio, 11
American Philosophical Society, ix, 31 n.80, 94
Andreani, Gian Mario: as guardian and patron of PA, 5–9, 12, 13, 94, 105, 106, 107, 109, 111; receives letter from PA, 92, 94, 97–99, 104–7, 109–12
Andreani, Maria Josepha (Cecca), 5, 95
Andreani, Paolo: balloon flights, 6, *7, 8,* 28; education and early life, 5–6; as ethnologist, 3, 21–27; health, 94–95, 105; as linguist, 24–25, 67–73; as meteorologist, 19; as mineralogist, 2; political views, 18, 94, 100, 101, 110; travels in Europe and Caribbean, 8–9, 94–95
architecture: Albany, 45; Halifax, 12–13; Iroquois, 55–56, 63, 65, *66;* New York City, 95; rural, 40, 41, 50, 53, *54,* 77, 85; towns, 41, 49, 50, 53, 86; Washington, D.C., 101
Ariosto, Ludovico, 80

Beaver Club, 23 n.66
Beccaria, Cesare, 19
Bingham, Anne, 90, 92
Bingham, William, 92, 103
Birdsall, Daniel, 39
Bowles, William Augustus, 12–13, 97–98
Brant, Joseph, 11

Brissot de Warville, Jacques Pierre, 17, 18, 20
Buffon, George Leclerc, Count de, 3
Burgoyne, John, 29, 36, 75–77
Bushman, Richard, 17–18

Canada, x, 49, 75, 97, 105, 109, 111–12. *See also* Montreal; Nova Scotia; Quebec
Castiglioni, Luigi, 2, 31, 43 n.23, 105, 110
Caulkins, Ebenezer, 60n
cheese, 92, 107
Cherokee Indians, 12, 56 n.52, 97–98, 100
Cincinnatus, 43
Claverack, 85
Cohoes Falls, 49, 74, *75*
commerce and finance: cost of labor, 17, 44–45; Hamilton's promotion of U.S., 101–2, 109, 110; land values, 53; manufacturing and mining, 39, 44–45, 52, 86–87; Nova Scotia, 100; among Shakers, 81, 84–85; shipping and transport, 39, 43–44, 47, 49, 54, 86; state of U.S., 98, 110
Condorcet, Marquis de, 9
Congress, 13, 14, 103, 104
Creek Indians, 12, 14–15, 56 n.52, 97–98, 100
Crèvecoeur, J. Hector St. John de, 17, 18
Croton River, 39

Delaware Indians, 55
Deluc, Jean André, 9, 37 n.12
De Pauw, Cornelius, 22
Desmarest, Nicolas, 2
Dublin, Ireland, 106
Duer, William, 14, 101–2

.

www.ingramcontent.com/pod-product-compliance
Lightning Source LLC
Chambersburg PA
CBHW030931150426
42812CB00064B/2732/J